What Do You See?

Time Then, Time Again

Jacqueline Jordan & J.E.

Acknowledgment

This book would not have been possible without the support and encouragement of several incredible people in my life.

To John and Elijah ~ J.E., Uncle Jerry St.Clair, and my beloved sister, Julie Jordan Huber—thank you for your constant presence and love. Your support has meant the world to me.

To my children, William, Angela, and Toby Turner— your encouragement and belief in me have been the foundation of this journey. Thank you for standing by me through every step of this vision. I honestly couldn't have done it without you.

A heartfelt thank you to my daughter-in-law, Cindi, for giving me the phone that helped capture the images that brought this book to life.

To my amazing granddaughter, Ciara—thank you for helping me turn my dream into a reality. Your light and love inspire me more than you know.

I am also deeply grateful to my friend, Alma Hankel, for believing in me, and to my assistant, Kellee Cullinane, whose guidance and help with Microsoft Word made it possible to bring this book together.

To my dearest friend, Felicia Jaekel—thank you for your unwavering support and presence. Knowing you are always in our corner brings comfort and strength beyond measure. Your loyalty is a rare and treasured gift, and your friendship makes everything better. We are endlessly grateful to have you in our lives.

Author's Note

This book is filled with joy, love, and the beauty of God and heaven.

However, my story began in a home where I did not feel wanted or loved. My journey has been a search for the love I lacked as a child.

This book reflects my discoveries: God's love is Real, even for those who feel forgotten.

I invite you to see this book not as a tale of my past but as a glimpse of the hope and love I have found.

About the Author

Jacqueline grew up with eleven siblings, one outhouse, and electricity that wasn't always on. Every day, they walked to an old mill to get water. These things shaped her early life. The long walks, carrying heavy buckets, taught her to keep going, no matter what. And even though the walk to school was a mile, it was a nice break.

Jacqueline couldn't remember much of her childhood; her memory was like sand slipping through the fingers of time. This profound lack of early memories was a bewildering void, and she desperately sought to make sense of it.

Years later, she had a powerful life-changing vision in which her uncle Jerry took her to heaven and beyond. When she woke from the vision, she quickly wrote of her experience and had it copyrighted initially in 1997.

This amazing experience fills her writing with wonder, as if she's seen something magical that most people haven't. It gives her words a special, spiritual feeling mixed with the reality of a hard life.

Preface

Sarah's spiritual awakening began with a dream—a gift from her late uncle. The clock on the bedside table read **1 a.m.**
Within that vision, she journeyed through a resonant realm with her uncle, who had passed on only seven days before coming for her.

Guided by unseen tides, she witnessed the interconnectedness of being, from the birth of luminous echoes to the dance of swirling currents, a tapestry woven with love. Ancient Voices revealed secrets of creation and the soul's timeless voyage. A reflective expanse showed her the depths of her being, revealing the divine wisdom within.

This vision ignited a spiritual transformation, leading her to embrace the interconnection of all things and find peace in the infinite rhythm.

You are about to enter the subconscious mind, where the laws of logic yield to the mysteries of fragmented consciousness.
Witness a journey through this realm, where such consciousness unites.

This experience, captured by the mind's eye as memory, offers a new perspective. The vision you are about to read occurs within these fragments, drawing you into its layered depths.

To enhance your journey through this vision, the images featured in this book were created using digital art tools designed to bring their ethereal beauty to life.

The story concludes with a future of wonder, a place of eternal experience.

Contents

Introduction

Time rippled like water before Sarah's eyes, materializing in a shimmering form: her Uncle Jerry.

He stood before her, the man taken only seven days ago, yet he was more than just the uncle she'd lost. He was an echo across time, a homecoming after an exhausting journey she hadn't even realized she was on.

Then, time fractured.

Long-forgotten memories, scattered like grains of sand, surged back into her mind. Things she'd struggled for years to recall now returned with stark clarity.

She felt the universe open before her, a vast and intricate tapestry, strange yet achingly familiar. She wasn't just Sarah anymore, but every version of herself stretching through time.

Uncle Jerry's childhood, events long before her own birth, played out before her in ghostly overlays—a past she couldn't have known but instantly recognized.

She watched a little boy pedaling his bike down an alley, oblivious to the dump truck barreling toward him.

She heard the screech of tires, the gasps of bystanders, and the hospital's fluorescent lights buzzing above his unconscious body.

She saw the moment when the nurses whispered to his mother that he wouldn't survive. But Jerry had slipped through time's fingers, as Sarah was now. He had died, and then he had been reborn.

Slipping her small hand in his, Jerry guided her into a radiant light. As they moved forward, Sarah felt the burdens of past sorrows lifting and being released into the ether. Time no longer held her captive. She was free!

As she moved into the luminous blue beyond, she expanded, encompassing galaxies, lifetimes, and the fabric of existence itself.

She understood now:

"Love is the thread that weaves the universe together, binding its grand tapestry of light and darkness.

In that moment, time collapsed into a singular truth. Sarah had always been here, in every time, in every place, in every life.

And she always would be. With that knowledge, she stepped forward into the infinite.

Sarah traveled the long road of darkness through what appeared to be a giant telescope. Confusion of time within time faded as Sarah drew nearer to the light.

With each step forward, she was stepping into the past. Sometimes, she even stepped backward, but then she remembered something important.

"Sometimes, painful memories can hold us back. However, it is possible to release the hurt and anger of yesterday with a little effort."

Some people dream of time travel, reliving cherished moments from yesterday. It's like replaying a favorite scene from a beloved book.

As Sarah approached the light, negativity dissipated, unable to withstand its brilliance. Preconceived notions of evil lost relevance, and darkness vanished soon after her journey began.

Although remnants of evil might have lingered, Sarah could no longer relive any traumatic experiences. Her visit was extraordinary.

She gained the power to pause indefinitely at any chosen moment, fully immersing herself in past experiences.

She could revisit her entire life as if reading a book. Once a book is finished, there is no turning back. It was an incredible journey.

The story's end leads to a bright future filled with wonderful surprises—a place where we can all experience amazing things forever.

Before this, Sarah could only recall her family as blurry images in her mind's eye. She was now experiencing their lives in vivid detail, with sound and movement.

Early traumas had erased nearly all childhood memories; her recollections were not mere dreams but new experiences—an unfolding, vibrant journey of precious moments to be lived as if for the first time. She did not understand why Uncle Jerry led her on this journey, but it did not matter. Her gratitude was boundless, as was her joy in reliving long-forgotten moments.

Chapter 1: Beneath the Morning Star

Revisiting her childhood with Uncle Jerry, Sarah found a time of boundless freedom.

She was always excited to go on an adventure with her brother, Eddie. An inseparable pair, they found joy in the simplest pleasures, their laughter echoing through the summer days.

The anticipation would build every summer, and their excitement was undeniable as they awoke before dawn, eager to embark on their fishing expedition. They would grab their trusty fishing poles, a bucket overflowing with wriggling worms they'd dug up the previous day, and set off on an all-day adventure, their hearts brimming with excitement. The morning dew, still clinging to the blades of grass, sparkled like diamonds as they walked towards the creek. The air was alive with the symphony of birdsong—a cheerful robin chirping from a nearby branch, a mourning dove cooing softly in the distance, and the distant cawing of a crow. A vibrant butterfly danced gracefully among the flowers, adding a touch of magic to the morning.

The creek was a tranquil oasis, with crystal-clear waters flowing gently over the smooth rocks. They wandered to the bridge where they liked to fish. They'd cast their lines into the cool depths, their hearts pounding with anticipation.

Hours would pass as they chatted, laughed, and waited patiently for a nibble. When they finally caught a fish, their excitement was boundless. They would carefully remove the hook, marveling at the vibrant hues of their catch, and then gently release the smallest fish back into the cool, shimmering water. As the sun began to dip below the horizon, painting the sky in shades of orange and purple, they would hurry back home before the streetlights flickered on, their arms laden with a basket brimming with freshly caught fish. A sense of accomplishment and quiet pride swelled within them as they hurriedly prepared for their trip back home.

Sarah loved returning to the creek with her mother and sister Judy to hunt for hellgrammites, a predatory insect used for bass fishing. With pants rolled high above their ankles, they would wade through the shallow water, searching for the elusive hellgrammites among the rocks and weeds.

Her mother, a hardworking woman with twelve children, wore her short, dark hair in a practical style that framed her face. A perpetual hint of weariness lingered in her eyes, yet she kept a quiet intensity as she scanned the creek bed, searching for the day's catch.

Judy, her mother's double in many ways, always had a happy, youthful glow. Her energy had a way of bringing joy to all of those around her. As she splashed through the shallows with her little bucket in hand, her bright

14

eyes would spark excitement as they etched happiness across her sun-kissed face. Their time together was filled with infectious laughter and the occasional shriek of delight whenever one of them stumbled upon a hidden hellgrammite pool. With nimble fingers and quick movements, they worked together to capture the tiny, wriggling creatures that called the creek their home.

All at once, the air around Sarah began to shimmer. She could smell the damp earth and hear the familiar humming sound of the old refrigerator.

She realized she was standing in her childhood yard. She was back home, just as she had always pictured it in her mind.

When she looked inside the old refrigerator, it wasn't filled with food. Instead, it held the wriggling creatures they had caught earlier at the creek. Everything was carefully packed with damp newspaper and ice, keeping the nightcrawlers and lively hellgrammites fresh for the morning's market.

This makeshift cold storage had been Sarah's dad's ingenious idea; a way to keep their valuable bait in prime condition. A thick orange extension cord snaked across the lawn, a vital lifeline connecting their worm business to the neighbor's electrical outlet. The deal was simple yet mutually beneficial: free bait for the neighbor in exchange for the consistent power needed to keep the worms fresh.

Just then, Judy's voice, young and bright, cut through the stillness.

"Mom said," she hollered. "Worms are fifty cents a dozen today!"

The door slammed shut again, leaving Sarah to her thoughts.

Fifty cents a dozen, she repeated silently, a small smile playing on her lips.

Digging for worms and sorting them into containers wasn't glamorous work, but it was their work. It was family work.

Just then, a dusty pickup truck rumbled to a stop at the curb. A man with a weathered face and a fishing hat climbed out.

"Got any worms today, young lady?" he called, his voice carrying across the yard.

Sarah straightened up, brushing dirt off her shorts.

"Yes, sir! We do! Fifty cents a dozen," she replied, her smile widening.

This was her favorite part—the exchange, the feeling of a successful sale.

"I'll take a dozen," the man said, pulling two quarters from his pocket.

He handed them to Sarah, his calloused hand briefly touching hers.

Sarah tucked the fifty cents into her pocket as the truck drove away. The work was challenging, her hands often sore and stained with dirt, but the shared laughter, the friendly banter with customers, and the feeling of contributing made it worthwhile. She knew she would cherish these memories long after the old refrigerator had rusted and the extension cord had been coiled away.

As her Uncle Jerry guided her, they strolled along the road through the gardens, pausing only when Sarah wanted to explore.

And then they found it, a portal shimmering like ripples in a pond. She stepped closer, peering through its frame, and gasped. While looking through the door, she was teleported to a place long past. She saw her dog, Rags, and then she saw herself swinging on the swings at her school. Rags had bright, sparkling eyes that seemed to hold stories from far-off places. He bounced around as if he could fly, always happy and eager for fun.

"Rags!" she called, her voice a hushed plea, a whisper carried on the wind.

It was a call across the chasm of time, a desperate reach for the vibrant echo of his youth. But he couldn't hear her. He was gone, not just from the backyard but from her world. She could only watch him through the window of years gone by.

Wherever Rags went, he brought joy. On the days Sarah felt down, Rags would curl beside her, offering comfort with his soft fur and gentle presence. His tail was always wagging, a constant reminder of his love and loyalty. Sometimes, Sarah considered him a guardian angel, sent to remind her that life was full of magic and happiness.

Whenever Rags' eyes sparkled with mischief, she knew an adventure was about to begin. Every day with Rags felt like an exciting new journey. Even simple moments like walking down the alley behind her house or playing fetch turned into grand adventures with him by her side. To Sarah, Rags wasn't just a pet; he was her best friend and a reminder of the joy life had to offer.

Then, she saw herself playing on the swings at the school playground with her brother, Eddie where the rusty chains sang their familiar song. As she swung higher, a delicate butterfly landed on the chain, its wings catching the sunlight and shimmering with a magical glow.

"Oh, look, Eddie, isn't he beautiful!" Sarah yelled out to her brother, her voice echoing across the empty playground of the past.

The sight made her smile even wider, as if the moment itself were filled with enchantment. She watched the memory unfold before her, a perfect snapshot of a sun-drenched afternoon. As she watched, she tapped gently on the window to the past, her fingertips brushing against the cool glass of the present world she was now visiting. It was a futile gesture, of course. They couldn't see her. They couldn't hear her. She longed for them to hear her, to somehow reach across time, to bridge the impossible gap between then and now, but the butterfly, Eddie, the swings, the whole scene remained locked in its golden frame, forever out of reach.

But despite her efforts, the sounds from the past remained muffled, as though the barrier between them was unbreakable. Her taps went unnoticed, and the moments continued, untouched by her presence.

WILLIAM TURNER

Stepping back into her second-grade classroom, Sarah was overwhelmed by a wave of recollection as she scanned the room, her eyes darting from face to face in search of the one she wanted to see. And there he was— her future husband—sitting at a small desk, his brow furrowed in concentration as he wrestled with an especially challenging addition problem.

He was so small, so serious.

Sarah's thoughts drifted, and she wondered if he could sense her gaze from this peculiar place where time seemed to stand still. A mischievous grin spread across her face as she remembered Bill's wildly exaggerated tales of their childhood escapades on the playground. He would dramatically claim that she had pushed him so hard on the swing that he had almost reached the moon!

Though Sarah couldn't quite recall the incident, the memory, tinged with laughter and joy, warmed her heart. *He probably embellished it even then,* she thought, smiling.

It felt like the room around her disappeared, leaving only the bright and colorful memories of their past together and the exciting promise of their future. Each of Bill's exaggerated stories and every moment of laughter highlighted the beautiful story of their bond: A story that had already begun, even then, in that small, sun-drenched classroom, a story that would unfold with vibrant, exciting energy years later.

She wanted to reach out, to touch his shoulder, to whisper, *"It's me, Sarah. We're going to have a wonderful life together,"* but she knew she couldn't. He was locked in his own time, just as she was locked in hers. She could only watch as a silent observer in the theater of their shared history.

Time seemed to advance over the next few years as she could hear the echoes of their adventures together, creating a picture of a journey filled with joy, love, and endless possibilities. The promise of their future shone brightly, casting a hopeful light over the memories that warmed her heart and lit up the path ahead. At that moment, everything else seemed to pause, allowing their love story to take center stage, ready for many exhilarating chapters yet to come.

Sarah and her Uncle Jerry continued their stroll through the sun-drenched garden. Like a gentle breeze, a quiet curiosity stirred within her, guiding her steps. She paused beside a Border Collie, its sleek black-and-white coat strikingly contrasted against the lush green lawn.

Gently, she stroked its soft fur.

"What do you see out there?" she asked, her voice a soft murmur.

The Collie's blue eyes flickered, and a thought, clear as a bell, echoed in her mind: *"Paths. Some clear, some hidden."*

"Hidden paths?" Sarah murmured, her brow furrowing slightly. "Where do they lead?"

The Collie tilted its head, a silent question in its gaze.

"Places you might not expect," it conveyed, a hint of mystery in its tone.

A warm, wet nose nudged her hand. A Golden Retriever, its tail wagging gently, pressed against her skin.

"Love" conveyed a simple, unwavering feeling.

"I love you too," Sarah replied, a smile gracing her lips. "You're a good friend."

Elegant cats moved through the flowerbeds, their eyes glittering jewels. A sleek black cat paused, its emerald eyes fixed on Sarah.

"You ask so many questions," it purred, resonating in her mind.

"Is that a bad thing?" Sarah asked, kneeling before it.

"It can lead to uncomfortable truths," the cat replied in its calm and smooth voice. *"But also, to... revelations."*

"What kind of revelations?" Sarah pressed, her curiosity piqued.

The cat blinked slowly, its gaze unwavering. *"Those, you must discover for yourself."*

In the distance, elks grazed, their antlers like branches reaching toward the sky.

"The wind whispers stories," one of them rumbled. Its voice was deep and resonant.

"Stories of what?" Sarah asked, her voice hushed.

"Of time, of change, of the earth's long memory," the elk replied, his gaze sweeping across the garden.

As the sun began to set, casting long shadows across the garden, Sarah found herself drawn to an ancient oak, its bark rough and gnarled.

"You've seen so much," she whispered, touching the weathered surface.

Deep stillness filled her mind—a feeling of ancient wisdom.

"I've seen the seasons turn, the stars shift, and the earth breathe," the tree seemed to respond with its voice, silently resonating within her.

"And what have you learned?" Sarah asked, her voice barely a whisper.

"That all things are connected," the tree replied. *"And that the greatest mysteries are found in the quietest moments."*

The tree pulsed with a gentle light. Its roots were thick and gnarled, reaching not into the earth but into the very fabric of existence.

They hummed with a quiet energy, a song of creation. In shades of emerald and amethyst, the leaves whispered not just ancient secrets but greetings, stories, and blessings. Each rustle was a word, each swaying a sentence.

Long and strong branches reached out like welcoming arms, their leaves murmuring, "Welcome, child. Welcome home, Sarah."

Uncle Jerry said, his voice a low rumble. "Come here, child."

They stood beneath the tree's canopy, bathed in an airy glow. The smooth and warm bark pulsed with memories, each scar a tale told in light and love.

"Look," it whispered, like the chime of distant bells. *"Look at all you have become."*

Sarah felt a tug, a connection not just to the earth but to everything: the stars, the light, the very air itself. The distant sounds of chirping crickets and rustling leaves were a symphony of welcome, each instrument playing a song of joy.

It's like... like coming home, she thought, a bittersweet ache resonating. *But...*

"I wish they were here," she whispered, the words catching in her throat, thinking of her family.

The tree's leaves rustled, a soft, comforting sound. *"They are here, my child,"* the wind whispered, smooth as a caress, carrying the voices of loved ones. *"They are always here, in your heart, in the light, in the love surrounding you."*

A knowing smile, as radiant as the tree's light, deepened on Uncle Jerry's face as he gently squeezed her hand. In that shared touch, she felt the enduring warmth of their memories, a bond that time could not diminish.

"Look at me, Sarah!" he exclaimed, his eyes sparkling. "Watch this!"

He began to dance, a joyful, spontaneous jig as autumn leaves in a gentle breeze. His face was joyful, moving to a tune only he could hear.

Oh, Grandma would have loved this, Sarah thought, her heart warming up. *She'd be laughing, clapping her hands.*

The thought deepened her yearning, intertwining warmth with longing. *If only she could see him now...*

Is there a way? She continued, her gaze sweeping the lush greenery and vibrant flowers. *Is there a way to share this?* She could only imagine her grandmother's eyes lighting up, her laughter echoing through the trees.

"This is... This is real, isn't it?" Sarah questioned, her eyes widening as she looked at her uncle. He looked... different.

A gentle flutter of invisible wings echoed around her, a serene whisper in the air. A warm sensation spread through her like the comforting embrace of a cherished memory, and she felt a profound connection with her uncle's thoughts.

He's happy, she realized, a wave of understanding washing over her. *He's truly, completely happy.*

The surroundings seemed to come alive with a radiant brilliance. The landscape transformed into a breathtaking tapestry of vibrant flowers; each bloom more colorful and exquisite than the last.

The ground, now adorned with lush, emerald grass, felt cool and inviting beneath her feet.

"Look at the apples, Sarah!" Uncle Jerry called; his voice filled with childlike wonder.

The apple trees were impossibly tall. They shimmered with an inner light, their branches laden with fruit that glowed like jewels—rubies and emeralds, yes, but also amethysts and sapphires.

"This isn't just a dream," she breathed, her voice barely a whisper. "This is... home."

The air hummed with a symphony of scents: blossoms, ripe fruit, and the very essence of joy, peace, and homecoming. A brook chuckled nearby, its water a mirror to the sky, holding the same blue. Dragonflies, their wings woven with rainbows, danced above the mirrored surface. And the music... oh, the music. It drifted in the air, resonating not just in her ears but in her very soul.

It's... it's singing to me, she thought, tears welling in her eyes. *It knows me.*

Each note was a word, a greeting, a reminder of the love surrounding her. The trees, the flowers, the light, and the air sing together in a chorus of pure, unadulterated joy.

"I'm home," she whispered, her smile radiant. "I'm finally home."

The music wasn't just heard; it was felt. It touched a place deep within Sarah, a place beyond words. It flowed through her like liquid light, washing away not just worries but the concept of worry.

"It's beautiful, isn't it?" Uncle Jerry said, his voice soft. "It's all for you."

"For me?" she echoed, her heart swelling.

It was a symphony, a caress, a whisper, a homecoming. Each note was a tiny spark of pure love. It was the gentle pulse of creation itself, a lullaby whispered by the universe. The air thrummed with the music's vibrations, a tangible presence, both intimate and boundless.

"I understand now," she thought, her eyes filled with tears of joy. "I understand everything."

It was an experience, a connection, a love song sung by the air she breathed. As she swayed gently to its rhythm, lost in its beauty, she knew this was her home. It wasn't just a place; it was a promise, a homecoming, a love that would forever reside within her soul.

A peculiar glow caught her eye as she wandered deeper into the enchanted garden. It emanated from a specific area, drawing her closer like a moth to a flame. Intrigued, she approached, her heart thumping a nervous rhythm against her ribs.

Like silken skirts brushing together, a soft, whispering rustle of leaves filled the air.

Distant birdsong, a melodic trill, and a gentle cooing blended into a symphony of nature, a calming backdrop to her growing anticipation.

As her uncle held onto her hand, Sarah witnessed another colossal tree, unlike any she had encountered. This one was not of wood and bark, like the previous one, but pure crystal, its surface shimmering with a spectrum of colors, shades of blue, green, red, and violet. Its leaves, each one a miniature jewel, glowed with an otherworldly light, casting multicolored dancing shadows on the forest floor. A soft hum, deep and resonant, rippled through the air, thrumming against her chest and stirring something deep within.

Alongside this was the gentle tinkling of crystal leaves, a sound like mystical wind chimes; their crystalline melody, a light, high-pitched dance of unseen currents and subtle vibrations, shimmered through the air.

Just then, her uncle spoke, not with words but with thoughts. "You were born with a special light inside," he said. "It can grow brighter when you share kindness and love, but remember, your inner light can dim if you judge others. Be kind and loving to keep it shining bright."

His voice resonated in her mind like a soothing melody, a warm, resonant tone that echoed without an audible sound, a gentle vibration directly in her mind, calming her racing heart.

It's beautiful, Sarah thought back, her thoughts echoing in the quiet space between them. It was a moment of profound silence punctuated only by the subtle hum of the crystal tree.

"But... why am I here?"

A pause, a moment of absolute stillness, where even the rustling leaves seemed to hold their breath.

"You needed to see this," he replied. "To remember. To understand."

"Understand what?" she asked, her gaze fixed on the shimmering crystal tree.

"The potential for good, for beauty, for love. It exists, Sarah, even when the world seems dark. This... this is a reminder."

Sarah reached out a hand, hesitantly touching one of the crystal leaves. It felt cool and smooth beneath her fingertips.

It feels... like home, she thought, a surprising wave of emotion washing over her.

The touch was accompanied by a faint, almost imperceptible "shimmering" sound, a high-frequency vibration that was more felt than heard.

"It is a part of you," her uncle confirmed. "A part of all of us. But it is not your time. Not yet."

The hum of the crystal tree intensified slightly and then faded back to its gentle drone, leaving a lingering sense of peace and mystery.

I don't want to leave, she thought, a sudden pang of sadness tightening her chest, a small, choked sob caught in her throat.

"But you must return. You have things to do, Sarah. Light to share."

"But how can I share this?" she wondered. "How can I bring this... this feeling back with me?"

The gentle hum of the crystal tree pulsed slightly, a subtle shift in its resonant frequency, like a comforting heartbeat.

"By remembering," he replied. "By keeping the light alive within you. And by sharing it with others, one act of kindness at a time." He paused, then added, "And perhaps... by telling your story."

A long-forgotten memory surfaced like a treasure from the depths of her being. A distant, eerie echo, a faint reverberation, began to build, a subtle layering of sound beneath the constant hum. Voices echoed through time, their tones blending harmoniously with the enchanting hum of the crystal tree.

"You're not supposed to be here!"

A childish giggle followed, a bright, clear, tinkling laugh, a sound like wind chimes in a summer breeze, a pure, innocent melody from a past buried deep beneath layers of experience and time. A high, clear voice tugged at something inside her—a warm, playful feeling.

Here, in this place, memories weren't just echoes; they were vibrant, almost tangible.

She almost saw it: a sun-dappled clearing, smelling of pine and magic, a gentle breeze rustling through unseen pine needles, a soft, whispering "shhh" sound.

A glowing crystal tree pulsing with an inner light, its hum now overlaid with faint, echoing laughter and a distant, melodic calling sound. This place, this heaven, held all time and all places. Who was she then, that child there, in that long-ago glade? And who was the voice teasing her, yet filled with such love?

The memory flickered like a candle in the wind, a soft, wavering "swoosh" sound, like a gentle breath extinguishing a flame, threatening to vanish before she could fully grasp it. She strained to see, to hear, to remember. Whose voice was it, calling to her across the bridge of time, across the expanse of forever?

A faint, almost pleading tone, a soft "Sarah...?" whispered on the edge of hearing, carried on the faint hum.

Chapter 2: Celestial Reverie

Sarah was a child again, ten years old and hiding under her bed, her heart thumping a rapid, excited rhythm against the wooden floorboards. She had just sneaked into her house after returning from New York while living with her older sister, Judy.

Now, her other sister, Kathy, found her peeking out from under the bed, her dark hair spilling onto the floor. Crawling out, Sarah emerged into a scene that felt both strange and comforting.

Once much shorter, Kathy stood before her and had transformed into a big eleven-year-old. Kathy was a year older than Sarah, and her smile lit up the room. Her hair, a cascade of golden curls, framed her little face, always filled with joy. Her blue eyes, deep pools of light, sparkled. It was as if an angel had graced the room.

"You're home!" she cried, a high-pitched, joyous sound that filled every corner, echoing pure happiness.

Time seemed to stop at that moment, holding its breath in awe.

A sudden, almost absolute silence descended, a moment of perfect stillness. The world outside the window simply ceased to exist; only Kathy and Sarah remained. A butterfly appeared, pausing just outside the glass. Its wings, catching the from the room, shimmered gracefully.

They clung to each other in a hug that stretched beyond time itself.

The soft sound of their embrace, the quiet rustle of clothes, and the gentle thumping of their hearts against each other created a warm, intimate soundscape. Sarah never wanted to let go, yet the thought of Lailonie, her baby sister, tugged at her heart.

"Where is she?" she whispered, her voice a soft, breathy sound filled with longing.

And then, there she was. Lailonie, not an infant anymore but a vibrant two-year-old, nestled in Sarah's arms. A soft, gurgling giggle, a sweet, childlike sound, filled the air—tiny hands patting her cheek. The love that flooded her was overwhelming, transcending even this realm of pure light.

Her uncle's words echoed in her memory: *"A child's light glows."*

He had seen it—that connection, that profound and sacred bond. Here, in a place where secrets whispered on the breeze and laughter echoed like music, their love felt tangible.

Echoed laughter met Lailonie's giggles, a balanced sound bending time. Sarah flowed into the beauty, her uncle nearby. Colors and moments merged into a vibrant symphony. Souls, a tiny universe of light, wove a seamless tapestry. A soft, shimmering "swish" sound, like a gentle breeze, accompanied the movement of the souls, a constant, subtle background hum. Sarah felt part of this cosmic dance, her soul resonating with the beauty and serenity of it all. The veil had lifted, revealing a glimpse of a never-ending story. Sarah suddenly found herself in a beautiful room that felt both strange and familiar. Her heart pounded with excitement as soft, echoing sounds—like gentle whispers—filled the air, carrying with them a sense of deep peace, like a distant, beautiful song.

Everything glowed with warm, colorful light, and a soft melody of tiny bells and drifting breezes moved around her, filling her with wonder. Glowing orbs of color floated nearby, each gently pulsing with its light. Filled with curiosity, Sarah leaned closer and whispered a tentative "Hello" to a small orb swirling with shades of blue and green.

As she gazed into it, a rush of color and emotion swirled within her as though she were looking into the heart of some deep and peaceful light.

Behind her, a tree stood tall, its long, strong branches stretching outward like welcoming arms.

The leaves stirred with a soft murmur. "Welcome, child. Welcome home," it said.

Then came another voice, low and familiar. "Sarah," Uncle Jerry called, his voice a deep, gentle rumble. "Come here, child." The light grew brighter, filling the place with warmth and color. Sarah felt pure joy. When it faded, she looked at her uncle, her eyes shining.

"I saw a little bit of forever," she whispered.

He smiled. "And forever saw you, Sarah. It always has."

Sarah felt at peace. She knew she was connected to something bigger than herself. A soft light from a mirror-like surface reflected many colors. The light hummed a gentle tune as Sarah danced. Her laughter sounded like tiny bells. Pearls appeared on her dress, sparkling with color. Sarah called for her uncle, careful not to disturb the glowing orbs around her.

"You'll see the light," he promised.

JACQUELINE JORDAN & J.E.

The orbs moved gracefully, making soft, whispering sounds. Sarah felt warm and peaceful. She trusted her uncle to guide her. As she danced, the mirror showed endless colors and patterns.

Suddenly, a bright light filled the realm like a burst of energy. Time seemed to stop. Sarah felt warmth and tingling, and a soft humming sound filled the air. It felt more real than any dream.

The light softened, and patterns on the surfaces began to move and change, telling a story of love and wisdom. Curious and amazed, she realized she was seeing the heart of everything. A sense of peace and connection washed over her as if she were home.

Her uncle's voice echoed, saying, "The light of the body is the light of the eyes."

His words felt deeply meaningful. Sarah reached out to him with her heart, and she was suddenly a little girl again, reliving a happy memory with sounds of laughter and nature, all mixed with the gentle humming of the present.

Sarah was two years old and perched precariously on the kitchen table. The wooden surface felt rough beneath her tiny hands, and the air filled with sugar's keen, sweet scent.

Her mother burst into the room; her voice was sharp. A sudden, loud crash as a chair scraped against the linoleum floor, followed by the echoing sound of her mother's raised voice.

"Get her out of that sugar bowl! Didn't you see her in there?" She scolded her sister; Judy then turned her attention to Sarah. "How many times do I have to tell you to stay out of the sugar bowl? I can't stand walking in sugar! Now, stay out of it!"

The harshness of her mother's words, a sharp, stinging sound, contrasted with the innocent babble of a two-year-old.

"But I'm not in the sugar bowl," Sarah protested, sitting innocently on the table. "I don't fit." Her tiny voice, a soft, innocent sound, was barely audible above the lingering tension.

"A child's light glows," her uncle's voice interjected as if from a distant, wiser place.

His warm, resonant voice seemed to emanate from all directions, a gentle echo that filled the space. Bathed in a warmth that soothed and illuminated her, Sarah stood motionless. A wave of warmth washed over her. It was calming and enlightening, as if a floodgate of understanding opened within her. Though a few words were spoken, Sarah heard music. A subtle, silent "hum" filled the air—a sense of shared consciousness, a connection beyond words. Music enveloped her, unlike any she'd known on Earth. A wave of heavenly music, a symphony of light and love, filled the space, a blend of harmonious tones that resonated deep within her being. It vibrated not just in her ears but deep within—a symphony of light and love.

As she listened to or felt the music, a wave of peace and joy washed through her, overflowing her soul. A wave of pure joy washed over her, making her feel incredibly light and free. A gentle humming sensation seemed to vibrate deep within her bones. At the same time, a delicate, tinkling sound, like the softest wind chimes, echoed in her mind. It was a clear, melodic "tingting," like distant crystal bells, resonating directly within her thoughts. This soft, melodic chime, almost magical, resonated within her. Light and sweet notes spoke to her heart, evoking a sense of tranquility and awe.

Her uncle smiled knowingly. *That's the music of your soul, Sarah,* he thought, it echoing clearly in the shared consciousness of heaven.

A clear message echoed in her mind, a direct transmission of understanding.

"It's real," he added aloud, his voice soft, "and beautiful."

And the very air around them whispered in agreement, *"Yes, beautiful. Truly beautiful."* A dreamlike whisper filled the air—a chorus of agreement, a gentle, echoing sound.

They closed their eyes and let the music wash over them, through them, becoming them. A sense of oneness merging with the music, a feeling of pure peace and tranquility. It was peaceful, calming, and a balm to the soul. Sarah felt a wonder and peace she had never known, not even in her most cherished memories.

Suddenly, a powerful voice was heard and felt within her heart, enveloping her in a warm, radiant light. It was the voice of God, a presence so profound, so loving, that she felt an intimate, transcendent connection, perfectly hers. Grasping her uncle's hand, she was swept away by an intense wave of love, joy, and belonging as if they were rising, drifting together on a current of pure beauty. The surrounding expanse, painted in soft shades of pink and gold, mirrored the beauty within.

Harmonious melodies, woven from light and love, filled the air, deepening the sense of peace and wonder. A soft, flowing motion, carrying the scent of blooming jasmine and other insubstantial fragrances, brushed around them. At that moment, Sarah felt an unspoken, yet utterly known, bond with her uncle—a bond that transcended time and space and was and always would be.

As they moved, the feeling of unity, of divine connection, intensified a sense of weightlessness, a gentle swaying accompanied by a soft hum that vibrated through them. This drew her gently towards a newfound understanding, not just of herself but of the intricate, beautiful tapestry of existence—a swirling kaleidoscope of colors and patterns, a visual representation of interconnectedness, accompanied by a soft, melodic weaving sound, like the gentle strumming of a harp.

This moment, this intimate encounter with the divine, would be etched in her soul, not as a memory but as a living part of her, a guiding light, a constant presence on her path of self-discovery, spiritual growth, and unwavering peace. A profound peace settled over her—the feeling of being enveloped in a warm, loving light, accompanied by a sustained, harmonious resonance and utter serenity.

In a sudden, dazzling flash, a sharp, bright flash of light, accompanied by a resonant "wheeze" sound, like a burst of pure energy, Sarah found herself whisked away through the very fabric of time and space, arriving once more in a new era.

Sarah sat at the piano, the cool, smooth ivory of the keys beneath her fingertips, the faint scent of old wood and polish, her fingers dancing over the keys as she repeatedly played "The Little One Said."

The repetitive notes echoed through the house, blending with the scent of pine from the Christmas tree.

The sharp, fresh scent of pine needles contrasted with the old house's warm, slightly musty smell.

"I'm sick of hearing that same note! Played over again," her mom yelled from the kitchen. The sudden, sharp sound of her mother's voice, a jarring contrast to the peaceful melody, was accompanied by the clanging of pots and pans.

Sarah quickly shifted to a new song: *"Do You Hear What I Hear?"*

The familiar melodic strains of the Christmas carol filled the room—a slightly more complex tune but still tinged with the tinny sound of the old piano. The Christmas song filled the room, but the tension lingered. Just as she found her rhythm of playing a different note, her brother Pat butted in, curiosity sparking in his eyes.

"Why are you playing with your eyes closed?" he asked, tilting his head in confusion.

His voice, a curious, slightly teasing tone, broke the rhythm of the music.

With a slight smile creeping onto her lips, Sarah replied, "I'm not *playing*, I'm *practicing 'I Can't Hear,'*"

Her fingers continued to tap out the rhythm of the note. Her voice had a playful, slightly mischievous tone, accompanied by the continued tapping of the piano keys.

Pat laughed, shaking his head. "You can't see what you're playing," he teased.

His laughter, a light, teasing sound, echoed through the room.

"I can see!" Sarah shot back, her fingers continuing to play. "If the boy with the glass eye can see, so can I." Her voice had a sharp, defiant tone, accompanied by the continued, slightly more forceful tapping of the piano keys.

"That's stupid," Pat snapped back. "Why are you practicing with your eyes closed?"

His voice had a frustrated, dismissive tone, sharply contrasting with his earlier teasing.

"Because I'm practicing 'I Can't Hear'!" she shouted, frustration bubbling over. Her loud, frustrated shout echoed through the house.

"You're crazy," Pat muttered as he turned to leave. His low, disdainful voice was followed by his footsteps retreating.

Their mother entered the room, her face a mix of weariness and annoyance.

"Can you please stop arguing? Just let her practice," she begged.

Her mother's voice was weary and pleading, filled with exhaustion. A sigh escaped her lips.

Chapter 3: The Offering

Sarah's heart swelled with love and concern as she recognized her siblings huddled together in the small, familiar space. A gentle, warm glow emanated from the area, a feeling of familiarity and closeness, accompanied by the soft rustling of fabric and the faint scent of old hymnals.

Their faces, usually alight with childhood innocence, were etched with excitement and guilt. Their whispered voices, a low, hushed murmur, filled the air, punctuated by nervous giggles and the occasional sharp intake of breath. The once comforting sanctuary of their church now seemed to be charged with a secret tension. The silence of the church, usually a peaceful stillness, now felt heavy with unspoken intentions, a sense of unease that hung in the air.

Sarah understood their pain. Their family struggled, and a birthday gift for their mother felt like a distant dream. The temptation to divert some of the offering was a siren song, promising a glimmer of hope in their bleak reality. The faint clinking of coins—a subtle, tempting sound—mingled with the hushed whispers, creating a soundscape of temptation.

Sarah's uncle stood beside her; his presence brought a silent affirmation. A warm, comforting presence, a feeling of quiet understanding, accompanied by a gentle, resonant *hum* that vibrated through her being.

Then, a divine message rang out, cutting through the children's hushed conspiracies. A sudden, commanding voice filled the room: ***"Give, and it will be given to you. Ask, and it shall be granted."***

The words reverberated with a force that carried unmistakable divine authority.

The children froze, their eyes wide with surprise. A sudden, absolute silence fell over them, broken only by their shallow, nervous breaths.

"Did somebody say something?" they all whispered, trying to keep their voices low, as confusion and awe brimmed within them.

It was a simple statement yet profound—a message the kids would never forget—a message of abundance, not scarcity, a universe where generosity was the norm, a power greater than material things, a power that answered the human spirit, a feeling of profound understanding, a sense of something greater than themselves.

The children, focused on their immediate need— a gift for their mother—couldn't yet grasp the whole meaning. The message promised much more: a harvest of blessings if they gave.

As they considered what to do next, the weight of the divine words began to settle on them. The words, moral responsibility, and a challenge began to take hold of them, in hand with a contemplative silence. It challenged their assumptions, inviting them to a deeper faith and trust.

Sarah was experiencing a confusing mix of emotions. She felt stuffed with thoughts and feelings, yet also empty inside, creating a struggle. Her heart beat steadily as she felt overwhelmed and a deep desire for something more. It was like her mind suddenly expanded, becoming huge, but she still longed to understand everything swirling within it.

Her uncle's words were soothing and helpful, like gentle rain nourishing her spirit. She felt a sense of gentle guidance and care, along with a soft, consistent dripping sound, like rain falling on leaves.

Her uncle acted as a guide, leading her through this unfamiliar part of herself. Each of his words brought new understanding, revealing hidden depths within her that she never knew were there. As understanding grew, it felt like layers were gently being peeled away. A deep peace took over her, a profound stillness from this newfound knowledge. This intense peace settled within her, and she felt connected to something larger than herself, a feeling that resonated like a continuous, harmonious musical note, surrounding her with complete serenity. She understood that something big was about to change within her, a journey that would take her deep into her heart. A feeling of excitement and expectation bubbled up inside her, like the start of an important adventure. This feeling resonated within her, a quiet but strong inner prompting towards something more profound.

Then, gently but surely, it was as if she was being pulled into another memory, another moment in time.

"Mr. Piano Person," Sarah whispered, addressing her piano like an old friend. She traced her fingers gently over the ivory keys, feeling their smoothness. "Are you lonesome tonight? Do you want me to play some beautiful music for you? Oh, how I wish I could get that music out of you. I know you have beautiful music inside of you. I just don't know how to get it out."

Her voice quivered slightly with emotion, reflecting her deep desire to unlock the melodies hidden within.

"I'm going to stay with you forever," she vowed, her eyes sparkling with determination. "So, you can teach me all the music you have inside you."

Sarah leaned in closer, resting her head on the keys, waiting for the piano to play.

"Please play some of your music for me," she whispered. "I promise I'll practice what you teach me. I promise! Please?"

Sarah's father walked into the room with a music roll. He inserted the roll into the old piano and began to turn a crank. As he turned the crank, the piano started to play a gentle melody.

Sarah gazed up at the piano, her heart brimming with hope and affection. Sarah watched as the keys picked out the tune of an old song; she heard her daddy play on his banjo, *"ONE SUMMER NIGHT."*

Sarah felt a surge of energy as her uncle's hands touched her eyes. It was as if a cosmic light was being ignited within her, spreading warmth and understanding through every fiber of her being. Pure and unconditional love enveloped her, expanding outward to fill the entire room with a serene glow. Suddenly, Sarah felt a change in the very fabric of existence. A subtle *whirring* sound, like a gentle breeze passing through unseen leaves, along with a faint *shimmering* sensation, as if the air itself were vibrating.

She opened her eyes to see her uncle, no longer just a thought or a feeling but a tangible presence, touched with a wraithlike beauty. The air around him seemed to gleam with a soft, iridescent glow, a subtle visual indication of his otherworldly nature. His hair, streaked with silver, framed a gentle face etched with the wisdom of ages.

Ancient wisdom and profound understanding radiated from him. In his hands, he held a photograph of a baby, its eyes mirroring the vastness of the universe. The photograph seemed to glow with an inner light, the baby's eyes reflecting a deep, cosmic vastness and a faint, echoing *twinkle* sound, like distant stars.

A profound connection pulsed through Sarah. A wave of warmth and recognition took over her, the rhythmic thumping of her heart echoing a deep, familiar pulse of recognition. She recognized the baby as a piece of herself, a soul yet to bloom, a potentiality waiting to unfold.

The image vanished as quickly as it had appeared. A soft fading sound, like a whisper disappearing in the wind, was replaced by the sight of her uncle standing beside a luminous, cloud-like form. It pulsed with soft, unearthly light and a gentle, subtle, pulsing breathing sound. It was pure energy surrounded by a protective aura of vibrant color. The aura shimmered with a kaleidoscope of colors, a vibrant display, and a soft, harmonious *chord* that resonated through her.

Awe filled Sarah. Wonder and reverence overwhelmed her, rising with a soft, echoing gasp. She was witnessing the birth and growth of a soul, a glimpse into the eternal tapestry of life. A profound understanding of the interconnectedness of all things, with a gentle, harp-like sound. Her understanding of the universe expanded exponentially, bringing profound peace and purpose.

Deep peace settled within her, purpose and belonging blooming as a sustained, harmonious chorus rose around her, utter serenity taking hold.

"The unity you feel is in the truth. The truth is in the tree of life. A child's light glows." The voice, a gentle, resonant echo, filled the space, a powerful yet comforting presence, each word resonating with profound meaning.

The voice continued to lead Sarah, each word a gentle nudge forward on her journey of self-discovery. Gentle guidance surrounded her, a nurturing presence drifting in with the soft, delicate rain dripping on leaves. As she watched her younger self struggle and grow, profound empathy took over her. Understanding and compassion rose like a wave, with a soft, sighing sound—a release of long-held tension. She saw the challenges of childhood with a clarity she had never known. Understanding and acceptance settled in, wrapped in a soft, resonant chant that vibrated through her being, a connection to something greater flowing through her.

As Sarah moved through her memories, a sudden clarity struck her: every moment, whether trivial or profound, had shaped who she had become. The realization made her pause, catching her breath. She felt a quiet vibration in that stillness, and a new understanding settled over her—sharp and transformative. It was as if the world had been reborn, vivid with fresh color and sound, and she stood at its very center.

Without warning, a brilliant flash of light split the air, followed by a cascade of sounds, her memories unfolding at once in a chaotic, beautiful symphony.

The sky was dimming now, heavy with clouds, and the first signs of rain were gathering on the horizon.

Then, with another shift in time, she found herself back in her childhood home. There was a gentle *swoosh* sound, like a shift in the wind, and the familiar scent of her childhood home.

The scent of freshly baked cookies wafted from the kitchen, the warm, sweet smell of vanilla and sugar mingling with the discordant music that filled the house. A chaotic symphony erupted: a wavering "Mary Had a Little Lamb," a cheerful mandolin twang, the trombone's resonant boom, a trumpet's playful toot, and the percussive clang of makeshift drums.

Seven-year-old Sarah, her dark pigtails bouncing, attacked the piano keys with determined glee, coaxing out the familiar tune, however, with a charmingly uneven melody. Her father, with a broad smile stretching across his face, accompanied her on the mandolin, its strings weaving a lively distinction. Upstairs, Bobby's trombone filled the house with a brassy rumble, shaking the windows. Sarah, unfazed, found a playful rhythm to match his boisterous performance.

Across the hall, Dixie's trumpet added a quirky harmony. Her puffed cheeks produced a series of high-pitched notes that, while imperfect, added to the joyful racket. In the kitchen, Judy and Ted transformed a metal table into a drum set, their impromptu percussion creating a driving, energetic beat. Spoons, forks, and spatulas became their drumsticks, creating a rhythmic clatter that vibrated through the floor.

Sarah grinned, her eyes sparkling. This was her family: a whirlwind of sound and laughter, a vibrant tapestry of music woven from their passions. The house pulsed with their shared joy, a testament to their love for music and each other.

Suddenly, the back door burst open with a loud bang, and Sarah's little brothers, Toby and Eddie, tumbled inside, muddy shoes and excited shouts filling the room.

"Sarah! Sarah! Come quickly!" Eddie yelled, his face flushed.

Startled, Sarah jumped down from the piano bench, her fingers lingering on the cool ivory keys, then landed with a soft thump on the floor.

"Where are you all going?" her dad called out, his voice echoing through the house with playful curiosity.

"Come on, follow me!" The boys yelled in unison, racing back out the door, the screen door slamming shut.

Then, Sarah paused and heard Eddie whisper, "Look, I found something in the yard!"

The hushed whisper, a secret sound, filled the air with a shared excitement.

He started running ahead to his spot. Sarah peeked around the corner of the house and saw her brothers huddled together; their faces bathed in warm sunlight. A golden glow lit their features as faint bird song and the gentle rustling of leaves drifted through the air.

"It's an arrowhead!" Eddie whispered excitedly, his eyes wide with wonder. "This has to be worth lots of money." His voice dropped to a conspiratorial whisper. "Don't tell anyone, but I'm gonna hide it in the wall to keep it safe," he added. He glanced around nervously, ensuring no prying eyes were watching, then grabbed Sarah's hand. Their hushed whispers, sharing excitement and secrecy, filled the air, along with the faint clinking of the arrowhead and a small rock in Eddie's hand.

A butterfly, its wings shimmering with iridescent colors, landed on Eddie's shoulder as if drawn by the excitement in the air. The delicate fluttering of its wings created a delicate sound, blending with the gleaming hues in the sunlight. Its wings caught the sun and shimmered like captured rainbows, drawing Sarah's attention. She smiled as calm washed over her.

In its silent language of fluttering wings and small shifts, the butterfly whispered, "Secrets kept —are treasures found."

Peace and tranquility drifted through her, carried on the butterfly's silent whisper.

They tiptoed back into the house, the old wooden floorboards groaning beneath their careful steps. The quiet creak, soft and steady, deepened the atmosphere of secrecy. Each creak seemed to echo through the now-silent house, adding to the delicious tension of their secret mission. Eddie led Sarah to their hiding place, a large hollow space in the wall hidden behind an old, faded picture. The room smelled of aged wood and dust, and a musty old scent filled the surroundings.

Eddie slid the picture aside with a practiced hand and nestled the arrowhead into the hidden cavity. Sarah's eyes sparkled, her heart pounding with the thrill of their secret mission. They listened intently, and a subtle *clink* echoed from within the wall.

Eddie's grin widened, a silent promise of more adventures to come. He replaced the picture, and Sarah shared a conspiratorial glance with him, their secret safely hidden for now.

Chapter 4: The Light Within

Joy bloomed in Sarah's chest, a sunburst of warmth that seemed ready to overflow. This wasn't just happiness; it was vibrant, electric courage. Once looming and sharp, the shadows of her past had slipped away, their grip no longer clawing at her heart.

Now, the world unfolded before her like a living canvas, awash in swirling colors. Butterflies danced through the air, their wings brushing against the moment like whispers of pure, unfiltered joy.

One, a sapphire-winged beauty, drifted down and landed gently on her outstretched hand. Its delicate wings trembled as if sensing the quiet wonder in her touch. Soft as a summer breeze, a voice brushed against her thoughts: "The path ahead is bright. Fear not the shadows."

A symphony erupted, not just music, but a vibration that resonated in her very bones—a chorus for her soul. Then, a voice, smooth and cool as river stones, flowed into her mind: "Walk while you have the light. Darkness will be your guide no more."

The world had shifted; the veil had lifted. It was like a layer of grime had been washed away, revealing the vibrant truth beneath. Sarah truly understood, with a clarity that felt like cool rain on scorching skin. She took a tentative step, a flutter of fear battling with a surge of exhilaration. Then, another step, back this time, a moment of doubt. A forward, a back, a dance of uncertainty. Finally, a decisive step forward, and she stood before her house.

The old white house, weathered and proud, stood like a sentinel. Its tin roof, weathered by countless storms, shimmered softly in the fading light. The porch let out a low, familiar groan, a welcome home in wood and nail. In the distance, the mournful wail of a train echoed through the dusk, a lonely, comforting lullaby that tugged at something deep inside her.

Sarah knocked on the door. The sound was sharp in the quiet evening.

"Who is it?" her mother's voice, laced with a hint of suspicion, called out.

"It's me," Sarah replied, her voice a little shaky.

"Who's *me*?" the voice demanded, louder this time.

"It's just me," she repeated, the words echoing with a strange emptiness.

There was a shift, a moment of disorientation, and then she was standing before another door, her hand raised to knock on her sister Dixie's bedroom. The chipped paint told a story: layers of lives lived within these walls. The train's whistle, closer now, screamed a warning or perhaps an invitation.

"Who's there?" Dixie's voice was muffled by the door.

"It's me," Sarah said, her heart pounding.

"Who's *me*?"

Clutching her worn dolly to her chest, she ran, her small feet flying across the yard in fading light. Her father stood near the weathered chicken coop, a crumbling relic of simpler days. Nearby, the bright red pump atop the old cistern caught the light; a vivid splash of color against the muted past, pulsing with the quiet weight of forgotten stories.

"Daddy, Daddy, look! Do you know who this is?" she cried; her voice barely audible over the deafening roar of the train.

"No," he yelled back, "who is it?"

Another shift, and she was facing her little brother, Toby.

"Do you know who I am?" she asked, her eyes searching for his.

"Yeah, you're my sister. Who else would you be?" he shouted, handing her a crumpled paper star, fallen from his school project.

The train's thunderous passage shook the ground, but Sarah's smile, mirroring the star's radiant glow, shone brighter.

The sapphire butterfly, a silent guardian, fluttered around her head, its wings a blur of iridescent light. It landed gently on her shoulder, its touch a whisper.

"You are loved. You are home." The creature's words, a balm to her soul, settled the chaos within.

Sarah's mind was a whirlwind of memories and sensations, a symphony of echoes and whispers. The questions of her childhood, the train's mournful cry, and the butterfly's gentle touch blended into a strange, beautiful harmony. Each step was a leap of faith into the unknown, guided by an unseen hand, a silent promise.

Sarah found herself in another moment from her past. She saw a bus filled with her siblings heading to Sunday school. The air buzzed with the chatter of children, their voices blending into a symphony of unmistakable noise. The bus transported them to church on Sundays.

Easter Sunday was the only day they truly enjoyed attending church, a special occasion that brought joy and anticipation.

With a sharp eye for color and texture, Sarah's mother carefully chose scraps from worn-out dresses, once flour sacks, lovingly sewn into clothes for Sarah's older siblings. Now, these pieces were destined to become something new and beautiful for the younger children.

The soft rustle of fabric filled the living room as she spread the scraps across the floor. There were no patterns or templates, just her hands, her heart, and the quiet confidence of memory. Her scissors moved with practiced ease, gliding through the cloth like they knew exactly where to go.

Pinning the pieces together, she arranged them to showcase their complementary colors and patterns. The gentle clinking of pins and the soft hum of the sewing machine created a comforting rhythm. Her fingers danced over the fabric as she skillfully stitched the pieces together, guiding them under the needle. Sarah and her sisters watched in awe, their eyes wide with anticipation, eager to see the final masterpiece. Each dress was more than just clothing; it was a testament to their mother's boundless creativity and love. The joy she found in creating something special for her children was evident in every stitch.

On Easter morning, Sarah and her sisters proudly wore their new dresses, twirling and laughing as they celebrated.

"Mommy," Sarah excitedly said, her eyes sparkling. "My dress is beautiful! And the bow is so big. I just love it so much!"

"I love mine too," said Kathy, twirling in her yellow dress.

The bus engine rumbled softly out front as Dixie declared, arms crossed.

"I'm not going to wear any dress anywhere. Thanks, but it's a dress—like, it's okay, but seriously, not for me."

Their laughter echoed in her mind, blending with the vivid memory of swirling, vibrant dresses. It all felt alive again; bright, joyful, and full of movement. Those handmade dresses were more than clothing; they were stitched with love and resourcefulness, each thread a quiet testament to their mother's care. Passed down through the years, they became cherished symbols of her ingenuity, worn with pride and remembered with warmth.

As the memory deepened, it shifted. The soft tap of shoes on the bus steps and the gentle rustle of fabric filled the air. One by one, the children climbed aboard, their dresses catching the light, their faces lit with excitement for the day ahead.

The bus door clanked shut, and with a final honk, the bus began to move, carrying its precious cargo of excited children and their shared sense of wonder.

As Sarah stood on the cliff of this extraordinary experience, she felt a profound connection to all that was. It was as if she were a thread in a vast, vibrant tapestry.

"The colors, the music, the love," she mused, "they're all pieces of a grand puzzle, finally fitting together."

And then, the tapestry began to shift, subtly at first, then with a graceful, unfolding motion. Colors swirled, patterns danced, and Sarah felt herself being gently pulled inward, drawn into its depths. Moments once faded sprang to life with vivid clarity.

The scene before her coalesced: a familiar sidewalk leading to her childhood home. Four-year-old Sarah, a whirlwind of boundless energy, hopped with uncontainable excitement. Her sister, Judy, thirteen, knelt patiently, chalk in hand, etching a hopscotch grid onto the concrete. Judy's encouraging voice and gentle guidance filled the air as she showed Sarah how to navigate the squares, their laughter a bright melody against the backdrop of their serene front yard.

"First, you put one foot down, then you hop! Then both feet, hop! One foot, then hop!"

Judy hopped slowly, demonstrating each step so Sarah could watch closely.

"Now it's your turn," she smiled encouragingly.

Sarah tried as she sang, "Ya take one step; now ya take one step; and take one step."

She heard her sister giggle.

"It's okay!" Judy giggled. "You'll understand one day. You'll just have to practice."

Uncle Jerry held Sarah's hand as they walked together through the garden, each step wrapped in calm and wonder.

Then, clear and sudden, a voice echoed in her mind: *"Come to me, and I will show thee!"*—a promise whispered like a sacred invitation.

Ahead, a path unfurled before them, glowing with color, vibrant and celestially bright, like a rainbow bridge drawn from light itself.

Clutching her uncle's hand tighter, Sarah stepped forward, lifted by the soft swell of angelic voices that rose around her in quiet harmony.

Uncle Jerry moved ahead, gliding as if weightless, his presence serene. His arms lifted skyward, and for a moment, his hands shimmered with an otherworldly glow, gently pulling her gaze upward toward something greater, something waiting.

"There, a magnificent angel hovered in the heavens, its luminous presence radiating a light so pure and brilliant it rivaled the sun. The angelic choir's melodies weren't merely beautiful; they carried whispers… whispers of love and hope."

Music had been woven through the clear, resonant notes of celestial horns. Sarah had felt the messages stirring deep within her, though their precise meaning had remained just beyond her grasp.

In that instant, as if orchestrated by a divine command, the angelic voices and instruments united, a surge of sound that resonated through her very being. The symphony wasn't merely awe-inspiring; it was a conversation, a story told in a language beyond words. It was a perfect blend of luminescent and celestial glory, each note a distinct phrase, resonating with the purity of the highest order.

Sarah felt the messages within the music growing clearer, like half-remembered dreams surfacing into consciousness. The lights, dancing in a mesmerizing display, united into a flawless, iridescent rainbow, each color a symbol, a key to understanding the symphony's profound message. She reached out, her hand trembling with wonder toward the vibrant spectrum of colors and the enchanting music surrounding her. As her fingers brushed the air, a powerful surge of pure, unadulterated love washed over her, filling her heart with indescribable warmth and joy.

She felt an overwhelming sense of peace and security, as if the angel's presence shielded her from every trace of fear and doubt. The air had been alive with the harmonious voices of an unseen choir, their melodies more than just beautiful; they had carried purpose.

"Listen, Sarah," they had sung, their voices tender and sure. *"Follow your heart. Trust your instincts."* Woven through their song were the clear, ringing notes of celestial horns, each declaring with radiant certainty: *"The path is open."*
A promise. An invitation.

A hush fell over everything—just for a breath—before sound rose again, not as noise, but as revelation. The angelic voices and instruments blended into a radiant surge, a wave of harmony that moved through Sarah like light through glass. The entire symphony unfolded like a celestial blueprint, every phrase a signpost, every chord a step forward.

"You have a purpose," it revealed. *"Find it. Embrace it. Live it."*

Sarah felt the messages resonating within her soul, igniting a fire of determination. The lights, dancing in a mesmerizing display, united into a flawless, iridescent rainbow, each representing a different aspect of her journey: red for courage, green for growth, and blue for wisdom.

The angel's words echoed through the stillness: *"Come to me, and I will show you!"*—layering the moment with an otherworldly weight.

Uncle Jerry held Sarah's hand firmly as a radiant rainbow arched above them, its colors gleaming like a promise. She looked up, her eyes wide, capturing the moment: a memory etched not just in her mind, but deep within her soul.

The colors stayed close together, forming a perfect roadway into the heavens. Walking on this pathway made from the colors of a rainbow was something Sarah knew she would never forget. This moment, filled with celestial light and music, became an unforgettable part of her being, a testament to the beauty and wonder she had witnessed.

The roadway dazzled with light and color, but beneath Sarah's feet, soft green grass carpeted the ground like the fields of her childhood. The familiar scent of summer filled the air. The ground was a vibrant green, red, blue, and yellow mosaic. The colors, though close, never mixed, each distinct and lively, like a fingerprint. It was as if a magical force held them apart, a perfect, colorful puzzle. As she looked around, Sarah felt a profound connection to everything: the grass beneath her feet, the light cascading from above, the colors swirling gently around her.

"You are connected," the voice whispered. *"You are part of something greater."*

The scene around Sarah was very peaceful and calm. The soft light made everything look dreamy. As she walked, she heard a gentle crunching sound under her feet, like walking on a gravel path. The air was filled with the sweet singing of angels, their voices like a soft breeze that made her feel peaceful and happy.

Sarah could hear the quiet rustling of leaves, like the trees were dancing to the music. She also listened to the gentle sound of a faraway brook, which made everything even more peaceful. All the sounds together created a beautiful harmony, making Sarah feel entirely at ease.

Each step she took was accompanied by the whisper of the wind, gently brushing against her skin. The sounds around her created a sense of harmony and tranquility. The angels' song seemed to tell a story that connected her past, present, and future in a beautiful, seamless flow.

Sarah felt a deep sense of belonging and wonder as she moved forward, her heart lifted by the enchanting sounds surrounding her. The world felt alive with the whispers of history and the promise of tomorrow, all carried on the gentle breeze of the angels' song.

Uncle Jerry wanted her to see another past event, and suddenly, she found herself back in school.

"When you look out the window, what do you see? Where do you go?" The question echoed throughout the empty room.

Sarah's eyes glazed over as she tried to find an answer. "I don't know," she said slowly, her voice tinged with uncertainty.

The thirteen-year-old girl stared out the window, her gaze lost in the gray expanse.

"I go to school. I remember sitting at my desk, staring at the chalkboard. I watch the clock tick away the minutes, waiting for the bell to ring."

Sarah's voice was soft, almost detached, as if narrating a memory she wasn't entirely sure belonged to her. Her teacher sat nearby, listening carefully as she continued.

Outside, rain splattered gently against the glass, creating a rhythmic, endless pattern. Beyond the window, the world blurred, gray buildings, hurried figures, and umbrellas bobbing like floating shadows. A quiet sigh slipped from Sarah's lips.

"I see a rainbow that shines bright with light," she said suddenly, her voice distant but certain.

Her teacher glanced out the window. "And where is this rainbow?"

"It's in the morning star," Sarah replied, barely above a whisper.

Time passed gently; the room held in hush. The rain continued.

Later, in the quiet office of her doctor, Sarah sat once more, hands folded, gaze low. He leaned forward slightly; his voice gentle but probing.

"What do you see, Sarah? Where do you go?"

She hesitated, her eyes slowly rising to meet his. The gray expanse still lingered behind them, but something in her was shifting.

"I... I don't know," she murmured, the words strange on her tongue. "I see the rain. I go to school."

The doctor raised his eyebrows just slightly, his tone still soft. "And when you're not at school?"

Sarah hesitated. "Home. My room. Sometimes I look out the window."

There was a long pause.

The doctor nodded slowly. "And what do you see then?"

Sarah's eyes drifted back to the window, as if searching for an answer.

"Nothing much," she said softly. "Just the sky. Or the trees…" She hesitated; her gaze was distant. "But mostly… I see the morning star."

The doctor's hand tightened slightly on her arm.

"The morning star, you say?" He tried to sound calm, but his voice trembled slightly. "Sarah, do you understand that the morning star is a planet, not a star?"

Sarah's eyes remained fixed at a point in the distance. "It's different," she murmured. "It's special."

The doctor's gaze softened. He leaned in, sensing the depth of Sarah's connection to this celestial body.

"Why is it special to you, Sarah?"

She took a deep breath, her voice barely above a whisper. "Because it's always there, even when everything else fades away. It's a beacon in the darkness, guiding me home."

The doctor nodded slowly, his mind racing with thoughts. He realized that to Sarah, the morning star was more than just a planet; it was a symbol of hope and dedication in her world.

Chapter 5: Seven Angels

The late afternoon sun cast long, dancing shadows across the meticulously manicured garden. Hand in hand with her uncle, Sarah breathed in the sweet, heady scent of blooming roses and damp earth. A gentle breeze stirred the ancient oaks, their branches heavy with vibrant green leaves.

Then, just ahead, a soft glow appeared, like a pearl nestled within the twilight. Suspended in the air, an angel stood, radiant and serene.

Sarah's breath caught in her throat.

Before her, one angel became seven, each radiating a unique, pulsating light: warm amber, extraordinary sapphire, vibrant emerald. The smooth stone path beneath their feet shimmered, transforming into a swirling ribbon of rainbow hues, each color glowing with its own inner light. A low, resonant hum vibrated deep in Sarah's chest.

The angels glowed like polished pearls, their halos— golden crowns—dancing around their heads like playful fireflies. They held staffs of pure, shimmering gold, the light merging with their halos to create a unified, breathtaking radiance that stretched high into the darkening sky. The air, thick with anticipation, shimmered around them.

With each graceful step, the rainbow path beneath the angels glistened, illuminating the garden with an otherworldly glow. A harp's delicate, crystalline notes drifted through the air, interwoven with the soft, silver tinkle of bells. The music, a symphony of pure, unadulterated joy, seemed to resonate within Sarah's bones. Her heart pounded in her chest, a mixture of awe and wonder.

"What do you see?" her uncle asked, his voice a low, reverent whisper.

"Angels," Sarah breathed, her voice a hushed whisper.

Seven angels stood before them, their smiles gentle and knowing.

A sweet, ethereal melody like the soft rustling of celestial wings filled the air. It was a song that tugged at her memory, a lullaby of stars and wishes, but the words shimmered with a deeper, more profound meaning.

"When you wish upon a dream, a hope, a wish, a golden gleam.
The heart's desire, a shining star, a wish fulfilled, not distant far.
A twinkling hope, a magic sight, a dream come true, a pure delight."

The angels' voices, a harmonious chorus, washed over Sarah, filling her with overwhelming peace and joy. A silent tear traced a path down her cheek.

Suddenly, the central angel stepped forward. His voice, a wordless command, filled her mind like a breath of fresh, invigorating air. The sensation of rebirth enveloped her, a quiet but powerful renewal stirring deep within. The world around her sharpened; colors grew more vibrant, and sounds became crystal clear.

The golden staffs vanished, replaced by seven luminous stars. Before her disbelieving eyes, the stars shone and shifted, transforming into seven magnificent white horses, their manes and tails flowing like liquid moonlight. Each horse carried a new angel, clad in gleaming brass armor, their faces resolute and firm. A thrill, a mixture of excitement and anticipation, coursed through Sarah's veins.

As they began to speak, the armored angels released a love so pure and boundless that Sarah fell to her knees, overcome by its force.

"I know you! I know you!" she cried, echoing through the silent garden.

The air sparkled with the sound of celestial bells, their delicate chimes like tiny, crystalline whispers. The angels moved past her, their wings gleaming like strands of golden thread, their presence pressing gently against the air. The Lord's strength radiated at her side like a pillar of light, unwavering and sure. A surge of wisdom and courage rose within her, assuring her she was safe.

One by one, the angels spoke as they galloped past.

"In the night, a plea sounded; when I answered, you called me Jessica."

"A silent plea echoed when I answered you, Sarah, you called me Jennifer."

"Even in the darkest hour, I was there for you; I pulled you from despair. You called me Johnny.

"The moment you cried out in the darkness, I was there. You called me Tabitha."

"When the thief of tomorrow appeared, you called me Sabrina."

"Your spirit shone; you called me Samantha."

"I was ever-present; you called me Dorothy."

Sarah listened, her heart swelling with gratitude and recognition. She had never been alone.

The angels spoke together: *"We were there and are here. You couldn't see or tell. We are now, and we are one."*

A blinding flash of white light erupted like a celestial lightning strike, and the angels vanished. The divine light faded like a whispered goodbye, and Sarah stood alone in the quiet that followed. Yet she felt no fear, only a deep, abiding peace.

Like musical gifts from heaven, a symphony of tiny bells surrounded her. The angels' song, a harmonious blend of voices, filled the air. High above, seven bright stars appeared, drawing closer, merging into a single, brilliant glow.

A second later, an even more intense flash of white light illuminated the sky. The air crackled with energy, the ground trembling under her feet.

The fading light gave way to a low vibration, a sound like distant bells echoing softly through the air. The vibrant colors of the garden dimmed, replaced by a hazy, red-brown tone. The air grew thick and heavy with the scent of forgotten dust and old emotions. A shiver, a mix of excitement and nervousness, ran down Sarah's spine. She stood at the edge of a memory, a place she hadn't visited in years, the sights and sounds of the angels' visits echoing in her heart.

"Come up here! I wanna show you something!" Sarah's father called, his voice a mix of excitement and gentle urgency. "Hurry!"

Sarah crouched in the damp grass, her small hands stained green from the clovers.

Each clover, beaded with raindrops, reflected the morning light like tiny, scattered jewels. The air, still cool from the recent rain, carried the fresh scent of wet earth and blossoming honeysuckle. A rainbow, a vibrant arc of color, stretched across the retreating storm clouds.

"What is it, Daddy?" she called back, her voice bright with anticipation, her small feet kicking up small sprays of water as she ran. "Do ya have something for me?"

"Yeah, I have something for you!" her father said, a twinkle in his eye.

He took her small hand in his large, warm one, and together, they hurried around the side of the house.

There, nestled in the damp leaves, were two tiny birds, their pink, featherless bodies shaking.

Sarah's breath caught in her throat. "Oh, my goodness!" she whispered, her heart overflowing with tenderness.

"Do you want to take care of them?" her father asked softly.

"Yes!" Sarah breathed, her eyes shining. She gently cupped the tiny birds, feeling their fragile warmth. "I'll take good care of them, I promise."

As she took a step, a butterfly with wings like shimmering stained glass fluttered past. Then, a clear and resonant voice filled the air.

It was her mother, singing a hymn, "On a hill far away..."

The melody carried on the gentle breeze and seemed to weave through the raindrops and the leaves. As her mother sang softly, golden lights danced and shone around her like tiny, otherworldly fireflies.

"C'mon up here, I want to show ya'!" her father called again, his voice laced with excitement. "We're going to have a storm!"

Sarah giggled, her feet kicking up mud as she ran.

"Do you have something for me again?"

"Yes!" her father said, his eyes twinkling.

And there, in the leaves, were two more baby birds, even smaller than the first.

"Oh, my goodness!" Sarah gasped, her heart swelling with love.

"Do you want to take care of these little ones, too?"

Sarah nodded, her face glowing. "Yes, Daddy! I'll take care of them."

As she gathered the birds, her mother's voice called from the porch, "C'mon over here, I wanna' show Ya'!"

Sarah ran to her mother, who held an eyedropper. "This is for the birds," her mother said, her voice gentle. "Don't forget."

Sarah took the eyedropper, feeling a sense of responsibility. As the first raindrops began to fall, they went inside, where a cozy box awaited the baby birds.

With each dropper of crushed worms she offered, peace quietly descended over her. The house's comforting warmth, the steady rhythm of rain, and the sweet calls of the birds surrounded her, lulling her spirit into stillness. It was as if a loving hand had wrapped her in light, carrying her deeper into peace.

She drifted, weightless and carefree, as if cradled on the softest clouds. In this tranquil space, awareness expanded. A luminous light flooded her vision, but she resisted its call instead of sinking deeper into the stillness. Time faded away as she drifted into the infinite.

Chapter 6: Thirsty

The world shifted abruptly. The soft glow and gentle sounds melted away, replaced by searing heat and blinding light.

Sarah gasped, disoriented. Endless dunes stretched toward a merciless white sun, its heat pressing down with unrelenting force.

"Sarah, come with me."

Uncle Jerry's voice rang out, steady and clear.

She turned, expecting to see him standing beside her, but the desert stretched on, empty and vast. His presence was everywhere and nowhere—a thread of certainty in the suffocating stillness.

Beside her, Toby's tiny hand gripped hers tightly. His steps were clumsy in the shifting sand, his breath short and quick, but he didn't let go.

Sarah's throat burned. Her cracked lips felt like parchment, her limbs sluggish and heavy. Doubt clawed at the edges of her mind—was there even an end to this unbearable heat?

"Toby, we can't keep going," she whispered. *"I can't."*

Her little brother looked up at her, sweat streaking his dust-covered face. His cheeks were flushed, but his wide, serious eyes held something unshaken.

"Yes, you can."

His voice was small, but his certainty was absolute.

Sarah's chest tightened. How could he believe that? He was three years old. Too young to understand suffering, too small to carry this kind of certainty.

Yet somehow, he wasn't afraid.

Jerry's voice returned, calm but firm.

"He's stronger than he looks, Sarah. And his strength isn't his alone."

Toby tugged at her hand, urging her forward.

"Walk, Sissy," he said simply.

Sarah swallowed hard, blinking against the dizzying heat. But Toby kept moving, pulling her along with him.

She followed.

The dunes stretched endlessly, the ground shifting beneath her feet. She staggered, exhaustion pressing down like an unseen weight, but Toby never wavered.

Even as his small feet stumbled, he pushed forward, his tiny fingers curled tightly around hers.

Then - appearing in front of them an oasis flickered into view, impossibly vivid in the sea of sand.

A woman stood at its edge, her face soft with kindness, her presence like an anchor in the burning landscape. She held a cup—water, clear and pure, untouched by sand or heat.

Sarah stumbled forward, drinking deeply. Cool, blessed relief slid down her throat, and she exhaled a long breath, her heart swelling with gratitude.

She turned to Toby.

His small hands were empty, his face serene.

"You never gave up," she whispered.

He smiled, his weary little face glowing with quiet triumph.

The desert began to fade, the vision slipping through her fingers.

Solid ground returned beneath her feet. The heat clung to her skin like an echo of something forgotten yet undeniable.

Ahead, another door appeared.

Toby released her hand.

Sarah looked down at him, confusion flickering in her tired eyes.

"Aren't you coming?"

Toby shook his head.

"No."

His voice was soft, certain.

Jerry stepped forward, placing a hand on Sarah's shoulder.

"This is where he leaves you," he said gently. *"The next part is mine to show you."*

Sarah hesitated, glancing at Toby one last time.

He just smiled—small, tired, but unwavering.

Jerry opened the door.

Sarah took a breath.

Then stepped forward into another memory long passed.

Chapter 7: Secret Thing

The walls of this heavenly room weren't ordinary. They glittered like stars, and Sarah felt as though she were floating. Colors glittered all around, each more breathtaking than the last. Deep blues swirled like the ocean at midnight. Greens sparkled like fresh spring leaves. Pinks glowed softly, like the sky at dawn.

Yellows radiated warmth, like sunlight filtering through golden trees. Surrounded by such beauty, Sarah felt calm and full of wonder, as if she had stepped into a painting crafted by the universe itself. The colors didn't simply sit side by side; they flowed and merged like a graceful dance. It seemed as though an unseen artist had blended the most brilliant shades, creating a living glow that filled every inch of the room. The space pulsed with this luminous energy, and every corner hinted at a secret waiting to be uncovered.

Sarah stood in awe, her heart brimming with peace and amazement. She caught the faint sound of a hum all around her.

"What's that sound?" she whispered to her uncle.

"Why am I whispering?" she asked again, her voice melting into the magical air, making the moment even more mysterious.

"This is a special place, and this is a secret thing!" her uncle replied with a knowing smile, his eyes sparkling with the same magic as the walls.

As he looked at her, something clicked deep inside. It felt like a hidden door in her mind swung open. Suddenly, she understood she was connected to the radiant colors and the shimmering hum, part of something far bigger than herself. A rush of excitement surged through her.

In that incredible moment, Sarah knew she stood in pure magic and mystery, where dreams blended seamlessly with reality. She was certain this experience would stay with her forever, a precious memory of a world beyond imagination.

"I need to leave you for a little while, Sarah, but I'll be back soon," her uncle said gently. He led her to another memory, and then he was gone just like that.

"A special place. A secret thing."

The words echoed in Sarah's mind, looping over and over, until she found herself in a completely different scene from long ago. It was a place where yesterday never happened, today didn't exist, and tomorrow would never come. A place hidden away, never to be seen again—or so she had thought.

Six-year-old Sarah, with her wide eyes sparkling with curiosity, waited eagerly for her grandmother's promised gift. At last, Grandma brought it out: a vibrant burgundy album, its cover adorned with delicate gold designs.

"Oh, I thought you might like this," Grandma said, her voice wrapped in an unsettling sweetness. "It's a special album. Just be careful, dear. I'd hate for anything to happen to it."

Her perfectly styled gray hair and the subtle edge in her smile hinted at something unspoken.

"And really," she added, her tone sharpening just slightly, "if you ever get upset, maybe find something else to... release your frustrations on, alright?" Sarah cradled the album carefully, feeling the cool, smooth leather cover beneath her fingers. Slowly, she opened it and found an old record inside. The cover showed Baby Jesus, wrapped in soft white cloth, sleeping peacefully in a manger, surrounded by hay and bathed in the gentle glow of a single star.

"Oh, thanks, Grandma; I'll take very good care of it, I promise," Sarah said, her voice full of sincerity and gratitude.

"Thank you, Grandma," she repeated as she darted off, skipping up the stairs.

She tried to stay quiet, but each step creaked under her feet, adding tension to her secret mission of hiding the treasure away.

Sarah hurried into her bedroom and made her way to the secret hole in the wall, the special spot, where she and her brother stashed their most cherished things. She waited until she heard the satisfying thump of the album landing safely. With that, it joined their little collection of love and memories—treasures they vowed to keep forever.

Stepping back, Sarah took a deep breath, a quiet satisfaction settling over her. Now tucked away, the album symbolized a bond with her grandmother that she held close to her heart. It reminded her of the love and care surrounding her, even in the smallest gestures. In that moment, Sarah knew this album would remain a treasured keepsake, a piece of her family's history, and a testament to the deep connections that shaped her life. She tucked the picture back in place, flashing the same mischievous grin her brothers always wore. Memories came rushing back, one after another.

"I'm five today!" Sarah shouted, leaping out of bed.

But Penny, her seven-year-old sister, shot her a sly grin and sang a teasing song: *"I know what you're getting for your birthday, and you don't!"*

"What is it?" Sarah begged, her eyes wide.

"It's a secret!" Penny giggled, running her finger across her lips in a *zipped* motion.

"You better tell me!" Sarah yelled, stomping downstairs.

Creak, creak, creak went the steps. "Mommy! Penny's being mean!"

"It's a secret thing," her mother said calmly. "You're not supposed to tell secrets."

Sarah's mind buzzed with curiosity. *What could it be? A doll? A pony? A giant lollipop?*

Suddenly, a butterfly with rainbow-colored wings fluttered through the open window, its delicate wings sparkling like tiny disco balls. It twirled in the sunlight, and Sarah stood transfixed.

The butterfly perched on the windowsill, its wings still quivering.

Maybe it knows! Sarah thought, her imagination spinning wildly.

She watched as it floated away, her heart racing with excitement.

Whatever the day held, it was going to be AMAZING!

Another door appeared, and—poof!—Sarah shrank down, now just two years old. Her little heart pounded in her chest like a frightened bunny's. The hallway floor felt cold beneath her bare feet, creaking softly as she tiptoed.

In the kitchen, Mommy stood with her back turned, stirring something in a big pot. The sweet, warm smell filled the room.

On the table sat a baby bottle—her baby brother's. Sarah's eyes went wide with longing. She crept over, snatched it up, and tiptoed toward the back door.

Squeak! The floor nearly betrayed her.

Ted, her big brother, was watching like a hawk. He saw everything. The air between them felt tight, like an overinflated balloon.

"What ya got in your hands?" he whispered, his eyes narrowing.

Sarah tried to hide the bottle behind her back, but it was too big to conceal.

"Put it back!" he hissed, his voice sharp and low like a snake.

But Sarah couldn't resist. She pressed the bottle to her lips and took a long, sweet, satisfying sip. The cold milk was perfect.

"Sarah!" Mommy's voice rang out, sharp and scolding. "You put that bottle back, or you're gonna get a whippin'!"

Sarah's eyes grew huge. *Uh oh!* She shoved the bottle into her baby brother's crib and darted back to the hallway, her heart thudding like a drum.

"I told you she'd hear ya," Ted said smugly, shaking his head.

Another door opened, and laughter rang out. Sarah was a little monkey now, hanging upside down from the old oak tree, her hair wild and tangled. Her cheeks were flushed, her eyes bright and full of mischief.

"I see you, sweetie!" her dad called, grinning with pride, ready to catch her if she fell.

"Get her down from there!" her mom shrieked, her face pale with worry. She rushed to the tree, her voice trembling. "Don't do that again! You scared me!"

"But it was fun!" Sarah giggled, swinging playfully.

"I know it's fun, but it's dangerous. Let's go inside and draw pictures instead."

Her dad helped her slide down from the tree, and her giggles lingered in the air as they headed back to the house. Just then, the rainbow-winged butterfly floated in through the door.

"Look, Mommy! A butterfly!" Sarah shouted, pointing excitedly.

The butterfly twirled in the sunlight, finally settling on the windowsill as if it planned to watch them draw.

Sarah's mom laid out paper and crayons on the table. Sarah climbed eagerly onto the bench at the red and white metal table, her eyes sparkling with anticipation. She grabbed a red crayon and got straight to work, her tongue poking out as she concentrated.

Her drawing became a wild swirl of colors, not a house, but a super-duper colorful mess.

"Draw your house like this," her mom said, showing her a simple picture: a square for the house, a triangle roof, and a circle sun.

"Oh, I can do that!" Sarah said, snatching up her crayon with excitement.

Judy, her big sister, perched on a stool, watching quietly.

"Are you still watching me?" Sarah asked, scrunching up her eyebrows.

"Yes, I'm watching," Judy replied, smiling.

Sarah pressed her crayon to the paper, drawing with fierce determination.

"Are you *sure* you're watching?" she asked again, glancing up.

When she finished, the page exploded with a rainbow of colors.

"This is great!" Judy said, her voice full of wonder. "Mom, look at the house she drew! Isn't she smart?"

"Yup," Mom said, beaming. "She's very bright!"

Sarah bolted out of the house and down the creaky porch steps, her feet barely skimming the wood. She raced around to the backyard workshop.

"Daddy! Daddy!" she shouted. "Look at my house, I drew! Mom says I'm bright! Am I bright?"

"Yeah, you're so bright, you just glow in the dark!" Dad laughed, ruffling her hair.

Time shifted again, and Sarah found herself alone, floating in an endless sea of pure blue. A single cotton-candy cloud drifted overhead, a lazy wisp against the vast sky. Then, a wave of golden light swept over her, warm and liquid, seeping deep into her bones and stirring something long asleep.

It felt like a forgotten melody, something her soul recognized instantly. Her uncle stepped out from the glowing light, his form shining, his eyes alive with energy. He seemed brighter now, pulsing with a radiant force that felt almost alive. It wasn't just light, it was warmth, a presence that made Sarah's heart soar. She felt weightless, brimmed with happiness, as though she might lift off the ground.

Golden light spiraled around them in dazzling arcs, like tiny stars spinning in a cosmic dance. Then, a figure emerged from the center of that brilliance, bathed in pure radiance.

Its movements were impossibly graceful, leaving Sarah breathless. Slowly, a soft shower began to fall, not of rain, but of luminous white light. It cascaded over them, washing away every trace of shadow and leaving them renewed.

Tiny, crystalline flakes drifted down from her uncle; snowflakes made of pure light. They settled gently on her, wrapping her in a delicate blanket. An immense connection swelled within her, like she was part of something vast and beautiful beyond imagination.

He stood silently by her side, and love surged through her; a tidal wave of pure, unfamiliar joy. It swept over her in waves, filling every inch of her being. The connection ran deep, resonating in every cell.

He gazed into her eyes, and sparks of energy crackled between them: a live current. His hand rested on her shoulder, and suddenly, a jolt, like a mighty wind, rushed through her. She gasped, breathless, her heart thundering.

Sarah was lost in wonder. Love engulfed her, huge, trembling, overwhelming. It wasn't just emotion; it was physical. Warm electricity coursed through her veins. Her uncle touched a glowing cloud that hovered nearby and spoke. His voice rolled out in a musical, unfamiliar language.

From the edges of the golden light, thousands of shimmering clouds gathered, their voices lifting in a chorus of that same strange tongue, swirling like a rushing wind.

The sound swelled, a surge of emotion, a symphony of love and power. It wrapped around her, protective and fierce, as if she were cradled in the heart of a storm.

She couldn't understand the words; her tongue felt thick and useless. But her soul was fully connected. She felt complete, whole—a perfect, seamless union that transcended anything earthly.

It was as though the divine had touched her, filling her with a love so pure that she never wanted to leave, forever wrapped in its grace.

"Where are all those voices coming from? What are they saying?" Sarah asked, her voice barely above a whisper, eyes wide with awe.

"We understand in part and see in part," her uncle replied, in a tone that was calm yet rich with quiet power. "There are mysteries beyond what we can comprehend— glimpses of truths we feel but cannot fully grasp."

"And through the seed, all the world will be blessed. The love you feel is found in truth. Truth is found in the tree of life. Listen with your heart; you will understand."

Sarah closed her eyes, focusing intently on the distant, otherworldly voices. Every part of her seemed tuned to their rhythm. Then it happened, a shift, a moment of piercing clarity. Suddenly, the meaning behind the sounds clicked into place, and her mind filled with understanding.

She knew. And she could speak.

"Uncle," she said, her voice ringing with newfound strength and certainty, "they say that 'through the seed, all the world will be blessed.' They say that love is found in truth and that truth is found in the tree of life. As a fingerprint, as DNA."

The ground shuddered under her feet, the air seemed to whirr violently, and a deep, ancient voice rolled through the space.

"The seed is more than just a beginning," it declared. "It is a testament to the resilience of hope and the unwavering strength of love."

The voice whispered of sacred truth, an unseen dance of faith, and a new generation rising.

"Those who believe will believe," it echoed, "and again, I say, those who believe will believe."

Brilliant lights—vivid, swirling colors—flashed across the room, then vanished, leaving behind an immense stillness. Sarah's mind spun; her eyes locked on a cloud-like shape ahead. It felt like staring through a veil, trying to glimpse a hidden truth.

Suddenly, an image emerged: Judy, her sister, gently cradling a baby. A soft golden light surrounded them, and Sarah could almost feel its warmth, could nearly hear the baby's tiny coos. The love in the air was tangible, a presence she could sense as much as see.

"How did Judy get in there with that baby?" Sarah asked urgently. "Whose baby is that?"

Then came a lullaby, a familiar, comforting melody, and her mother's tender voice floated through the air. Every note stirred deep memories, bringing tears to Sarah's eyes. It felt as though her mother was singing directly to her heart.

"You called him Jamie," her uncle said gently.

"I don't know that baby," Sarah replied, confusion flashing across her face. "Is it Judy's? I saw a picture of a baby like that."

"Judy's baby passed when he was six months old," her uncle said, his voice heavy with sadness.

Sarah's heart clenched. *Such a tiny life.* Yet the lullaby continued, *"Amazing grace, how sweet the sound..."* Its soft strains filled the room, carrying the scent of summer air and the quiet rustle of leaves.

"How can Judy be with her baby now if he died so many years ago?" Sarah asked, her voice shaking.

"In this place, time doesn't work the same way," her uncle said, his eyes full of kindness.

"Love creates bonds that transcend time and space. They are together because their love connects them, even beyond the physical world."

Sarah felt a bittersweet ache mixed with comfort. The quiet voices and lullaby blended into a perfect stillness, making the vision feel achingly real.

"This is the time, Holy Spirit," her uncle said. "This is the right time."

The singing continued: *"Twas grace that taught my heart to fear and grace my fears relieved."*

The melody pulsed alongside their heartbeats, creating a sacred moment where past and present intertwined.

Thousands of voices rose, joining the song, a tapestry of sound that felt both human and divine. Each voice stood out yet harmonized, like the delicate chime of distant bells. Sarah felt it deep within her, a masterful weaving of spirit and sound.

"It was Grace that brought me safe thus far, and Grace will lead me home."

The voices melded seamlessly, lifting faith and hope sky-high. The moment radiated pure grace, a stirring reminder of love's enduring strength and the promise of eternal homecoming.

Sarah sat silently, her thoughts spinning like leaves caught in a breeze. Slowly, her mind began to settle, and a quiet clarity took shape, a feeling that anything was possible, that the future was wide open.

Today was now; tomorrow, just a dream—a place of endless possibility.

The wraithlike voices and glistening lights around her created a vivid, all-encompassing experience, filling Sarah with an unfamiliar but deep peace. Then, suddenly, she tumbled backward through time, landing in a long-forgotten memory. Sarah hunched over her desk, her brow furrowed in concentration, her school papers a blur of letters and numbers. The classroom buzzed with noise, but she pressed her hands over her ears, determined to block it out.

She focused hard on the page, but the words seemed to dance and shift, refusing to stay still.

Ms. McGee leaned over her shoulder, her voice a mix of surprise and curiosity. "Look! You got all the answers right!" She pointed to Sarah's spelling sheet, where the O's in the word "look" were decorated with tiny, hand-drawn eyeballs.

Ms. McGee even wrote "look" at the top of the page again, this time making the O's extra-large with playful eyes, to highlight Sarah's effort.

Sarah blinked, puzzled. "Right?" she asked.

"Yes, right. You spelled the word correctly. But... why the eyes?"

Sarah tilted her head, thinking. "Well, you said *look*, so I made them *look*."

To her, "look" wasn't just reading, it was a command to *see*.

Ms. McGee guided Sarah to the front of the room, pointing to a large spelling poster. "These are your spelling words. *Look* means to use your eyes to *read* something, like this word on the paper."

Sarah glanced from the poster back to her paper, then up at the poster again. "Oh! You mean *look* like... reading? Not *look* like... making the letters look *back*?"

Ms. McGee smiled warmly. "Exactly. *Look* like reading. And I have to say, those are some of the most creative 'O's I've ever seen. I even made the eyes bigger at the top of your page to show how well you did."

She pointed to another word. "Sarah, what does *emit* mean?"

Sarah's brow creased. "I don't... see it."

Ms. McGee held the paper up to a mirror. "Watch. When I hold it like this, *emit* becomes... *time*."

She watched Sarah's expression closely. "Your mind sees words in reflections, doesn't it? You notice patterns and shapes, but not always the meanings we expect."

Sarah nodded slowly. "Like... backward?"

"Not exactly backward," Ms. McGee said gently. "More like a mirror image. It's a unique way of seeing. And it's *not* weird."

"My brother Pat says my head is screwed on backward," Sarah muttered. "Kids think I'm weird."

Ms. McGee rested a comforting hand on Sarah's shoulder. "No, Sarah. You're special. And if you're unsure what something means, just ask for help."

Sarah brightened. "Okay!" She smiled.

"Show your mom these papers. And remember, when you write, keep your letters going left to right—just like when you read a book."

As Sarah gathered her papers, a butterfly with glittery wings fluttered in, landing gently on her desk; a quiet, beautiful sign. She felt proud and eager to show her mom. But somewhere between the front door and the kitchen, her papers vanished.

"Oh no!" Sarah cried out. "I lost them!"

"What's wrong?" her mom asked, concerned.

"My papers! The teacher drew eyes on them!"

"What do they look like?"

"The teacher made big eyes on my paper so I could see!"

"I think you came from Mars," her brother Ted snickered.

"I didn't come from Mars! The stork brought me."

"The stork dropped you on your head or at the wrong house," Ted teased.

"Stop it!" Mom scolded.

Sarah turned to her mom, eyes wide. "Did the stork drop me at the wrong house?"

"There's no stork!" her other brother Pat declared.

"Yes, there is!" Sarah insisted.

Her mom glanced between Sarah and her brothers.

"Sarah, I'll go talk to Ms. McGee tomorrow. She understands how you see things, and maybe she can make copies of your work. I'll also talk to her about how we can help you with your reading at home—and how we can help your brothers understand that everyone thinks differently."

The next day, Sarah and her mom met with Ms. McGee. Together, they devised an idea: a special book of Sarah's unique word interpretations, a "Mirror Word Book," as they called it.

Sarah felt a stronger sense of belonging and a little less like her head was on backward.

Suddenly, her uncle flashed into her thoughts, and she was taken away. A voice, soft as a feather, echoed deep inside her.

"All bodies are not the same bodies," it declared.

And like a leaf caught in the wind, she was carried to another place, another moment in time.

Sarah sat at her desk, fidgeting with her pencil, her mind a swirl of thoughts.

"Class," the teacher said, "did you all bring your ears today?"

"I did, I did!" Sarah exclaimed, holding up her fluffy earmuffs with excitement.

A ripple of giggles passed through the room. Sarah turned, expecting to see others wearing earmuffs too, but everyone just stared. A blush crept over her cheeks as she quickly stuffed the earmuffs back into her desk.

"Okay, class. Zip your mouths and open your ears. We've practiced all week for today. You'll fill in just one space for each question. Use this special pencil. If you don't know the answer, skip it and come back later. Any questions?"

The teacher smiled and continued, "When everyone's finished, I have a beautiful red apple for each of you. One, two, three... go!"

Suddenly, a brilliant white light engulfed Sarah, blinding and overwhelming. The classroom disappeared, replaced by a radiant, otherworldly glow.

Before her stood her uncle, transformed. His figure gleamed, and his eyes shone with a wisdom that seemed beyond human. He wasn't just her uncle now; he was a being of pure light.

He leaned closer, and though his lips moved, the words bypassed her ears, speaking directly to her spirit. He shared secrets of a hidden world, a realm brimming with magic and wonder.

"You are chosen, Sarah," he whispered, "a vessel for the unseen."

He told her she could pierce the veil of time and glimpse events yet to unfold. If she braved the trials ahead, she would be granted the Tree of Life, a source of eternal wisdom and strength.

But she wasn't alone. Soon, a celestial light would awaken hearts everywhere, stirring a deep awareness across humanity.

He urged her to lead, to become a guiding star. "For in your purity and kindness," he explained, "lies the key to unlocking the magic waiting for the world."

Then, a breathtaking vision unfolded. Vibrant lights swirled around her, weaving intricate patterns in the air like living rainbows. Beautiful music, a celestial symphony, poured over her, soothing and uplifting all at once.

Her uncle began to sing. His rich and melodic voice resonated deep within her, carrying ancient secrets and infinite love. Suddenly, Sarah was surrounded by glowing faces, each shining like a tiny star, radiating pure joy. Bright, infectious laughter rang out, a chorus of delight. Overhead, a rainbow blazed across the sky, dazzling in its brilliance. Warm, gentle rain began to fall, each drop glistening like a tiny blessing. Sarah felt weightless, as if lifted by invisible hands.

Then, without warning, the world tilted. Everything lurched. She was falling, tumbling through the air. The laughter faded, replaced by rushing wind.

She landed with a soft thud on an unfamiliar surface, the impact jarring her senses. It felt like waking from a vivid dream, her mind still overwhelmed with echoes of light and joy. Disoriented, she blinked, trying to process where she was.

"Sarah," her uncle said, appearing beside her as though out of thin air. "I'll show you everything."

Chapter 8: The Haunting

Sarah, who had just turned four, dreamed of The Wizard of Oz. On the television screen, an angel appeared, shimmering with golden light.

"Hello, Sarah," she chimed, her voice sparkling like tiny bells. "Would you like to join the movie?"

Sarah's eyes widened with excitement. "Yes!" she agreed eagerly.

Instantly, she was soaring on a rainbow, the wind whipping playfully through her hair. The angel smiled and presented her with dazzling ruby-red slippers.

"These are for you," the angel said kindly. "A gift to remember this adventure. You can keep them forever."

Overjoyed, Sarah clutched the slippers, watching as their inner light flickered and gleamed. The angel explained that they were magical and could grant any wish. But suddenly, a pang of guilt tugged at Sarah's heart. She thought of her sister, despite Penny often being unkind, Sarah wanted to share the slippers with her.

The angel encouraged her to put them on, but Sarah hesitated, feeling selfish. The angel's smile remained gentle, and after a moment, Sarah gave in and slipped her feet into the glittering shoes.

To her horror, the beautiful ruby slippers transformed into ugly, muddy blue ones the moment they touched her feet. Panic gripped her. The magical gift had become a cruel trick: a trap.

The bright, vibrant world of her dream crumbled into a nightmare. The colors drained away, replaced by a bleak, colorless landscape. Sinister, grotesque, and menacing shapes moved in the shadows. Overhead, a massive purple monster soared, its single, unblinking eye staring down at her, a jagged horn slicing through the gloom.

The air teemed with eerie sounds: dead leaves crackling underfoot, distant, mournful howls, and low, threatening whispers. Even the once-radiant rainbow now loomed dark and menacing, casting twisted shadows across the ground.

Terrified, Sarah cried out, begging to go home.

"Jesus, help me!" she screamed, her voice shaking.

But the witch's cruel voice echoed in the darkness, her words sharp as ice.

"No one wants you," she sneered. Each word felt like a dagger, cold and cutting.

Fear swallowed Sarah whole. She sobbed and pleaded, desperate to escape. The witch's cackling laughter rang out, filling the air like poison.

But then, through sheer willpower, Sarah summoned her courage. Clicking her heels together, she focused with all her might: There's no place like home.

The witch howled with laughter as the monsters crept closer, their snarls echoing around her.

"There is no Jesus, you filthy child! The promise you made was to me! Now I own you!"

"Jesus, take me home!" Sarah cried, her voice breaking with fear.

She awoke with a start, shaking, her skin clammy with cold sweat and her heart racing. Moonlight spilled across her bedroom walls, casting strange shadows that seemed to move and stretch.

She lay frozen, her mind still tangled in the nightmare. Every detail lingered: the witch's voice, the monsters, the terrible darkness.

"What's wrong?" Penny mumbled sleepily from her bed.

"I had a bad dream," Sarah whispered, her voice trembling.

Penny rolled over with a smirk.

"Too bad there wasn't a monster there," she teased. "I was hoping he'd eat you up!"

Stung and still scared, Sarah pulled the blanket over her head and whispered a prayer for protection. Eventually, her fear faded, and sleep claimed her once more.

When she woke again, the world had changed. Soft morning light filled her room, golden and gentle. A calm, peaceful feeling settled over her as she seemed to float high above the earth.

Jesus stood before her, radiant, his eyes kind.

"I give you my promise for being faithful and believing," he said, his voice warm and soothing.

He placed a helmet on her head and a breastplate across her chest.

"You will wear these until..." His voice trailed off, full of promise and mystery. "I also give you a spirit to forget yesterday, until..." He continued, his words carrying profound impact.

"You believe in me, and I believe in you. The love you give me will reside within you, and I am with you also. You follow me, and I will follow you also. You will not see me for a while, but you will see me again. For I am in you, and you will be in me."

The vision gently faded, and Sarah found herself back in her bed. But her heart was calm this time, with quiet courage and a deep, lasting peace.

Chapter 9: A Child's Perspective

Little Sarah scrunched her nose in disgust, wriggling under the thick, gooey tar pack that lay heavy and warm on her chest. She hated the feeling of the dark, viscous goop seeping into her nightgown.

"Mommy, it smells yucky," she whined, wrinkling her nose in protest. Her eyes darted to her little brother, Randy, and she burst out giggling.

"He smells yucky too!" she declared, finding humor in the messy situation.

She leaned closer to Randy, giggling as she waved her hand before her nose, exaggerating the smell.

Suddenly, Randy scowled and lashed out with a quick pinch to her arm.

"Ouch!" she shrieked, jerking back and clutching her arm, her face twisting in surprise and indignation.

Their mother stepped closer, concern softening her features.

"Randy, be nice to your sister," she said gently. "I know it doesn't smell good," she added, smoothing Sarah's hair, "but it's to keep you safe. You have to wear it."

Sarah rubbed her arm where Randy's little fingers had left their mark, her lips pouting. But the moment of sulking quickly dissolved into giggles again as she watched Randy grimace dramatically, his nose scrunched tight against the tar's awful smell.

Randy crossed his arms stubbornly, scowling.

"But it smells so bad!"

"I know it does," their mother agreed. "But sometimes we have to put up with things we don't like to stay safe and healthy."

"How much longer?" Randy asked, his voice muffled by the thick, smelly pack strapped to him.

"You'll wear it until..." Their mother paused, her eyes flicking to their father, who had just walked into the room with a sympathetic smile.

"But, Mom," Sarah whined, persistently, "yesterday you said tomorrow..."

"Forget yesterday," her mother cut in, her tone suddenly firm.

Sarah's brow furrowed as she turned to her father.

"Daddy, Mom said yesterday we could take this off tomorrow, and it's tomorrow."

Her mother sighed in frustration.

"Would you just forget yesterday?" she exclaimed.

Her father knelt beside her, his tone soothing and patient.

"It's not tomorrow; it's today," he corrected gently. "Tomorrow never comes. It's always today."

He carefully placed a hat on Sarah's head, securing it snugly. Sarah, despite her earlier complaints, gave a slight nod.

"Okay," she mumbled, her voice muffled slightly by the hat's fabric.

Her father gave her a reassuring smile.

"Believe me, you'll only wear it until..." He glanced at her mother, his voice laced with a hopeful note. "Tomorrow? Maybe."

Sarah's eyes lit up, mischief flashing behind her serious gaze. "Tomorrow, tomorrow... But tomorrow never comes," she echoed thoughtfully, playing with her father's words.

As she spoke, a strange hush took over the room. Sarah felt a tingling sensation in her chest, as though something unseen was listening, waiting. Then, without warning, a soft, pulsing whisper seemed to rise from the glowing tar pack itself, enveloping the room with a mysterious presence.

"Will you do these things for me? Will you do these things for me? Believe in the power..."

Sarah's heart fluttered with excitement. She reached out instinctively to touch it, but instead of cold or sticky tar, her hand met a warm, soothing sensation that seemed to spread through her chest.

Suddenly, a gentle tug at her hand made her gasp. She looked down, eyes wide, and saw a tiny, glowing figure standing beside her bed.

The figure shimmered, made entirely of light, its surface iridescent and alive. Its sparkling eyes twinkled with playful kindness.

"I'm here to help you," the figure said, a melodious chime filling the room like soft music.

"I'm the guardian of *tomorrow*."

Sarah's breath caught, her eyes growing even wider in wonder.

What is tomorrow like? she thought, her mind racing with questions.

"It's a place of hope and healing," the figure answered gently, responding to her thoughts. "A place where you'll be free from pain and sickness."

A wave of joy swept over Sarah, making her heart feel light.

"Can I go there?" she asked, her voice trembling with excitement. Every part of her eagerly awaited the answer.

Then, without warning, the atmosphere changed, soft and peaceful, as Jesus's presence took over the room. The calm deepened, and together they drifted into sleep, wrapped in quiet comfort.

Time seemed to stretch and blur. Suddenly, the present faded away, replaced by a vivid memory, so sharp and sudden it hit Sarah like a wave. She was three again, her small hands shaking as she clutched her doll close, holding it like a lifeline.

"Mommy! Mommy! Look at my dolly!" Sarah cried out, her voice high and desperate, tears welling in her eyes.

The room around her felt still, every sound echoing as her small world collapsed. Her beloved doll, once a source of endless comfort, now lay broken in her arms. Its tiny arm hung loose, detached, and limp.

"She's broken," Sarah whispered, her voice cracking.

She gazed at the doll, cradling it as though it were a part of herself.

Her mother knelt beside her, examining the damage with gentle hands.

"Can you fix her?" Sarah asked, her eyes pleading.

Her mother looked closely. "What happened to her arm?"

Through sobs, Sarah explained, "Tony the pony stepped on it and broke it off."

Her older brother, Bobby, stepped in, holding up the smashed doll arm.

"I know what to do!" Sarah's other sister, Kathy, chirped brightly. "There's an old doll in the attic with no legs. I'll get it for you; you can use her arm."

Hope sparked in Sarah's eyes.

"When will she be fixed?" she asked eagerly, her tears beginning to dry.

"In a little while," her mother promised with a reassuring smile. "Now go play, and she'll be all better soon."

Sarah nodded, clutching her doll tightly to her chest as she ran off. But as she hurried out the door, a strange, chilling whisper drifted through her mind: *"In a little while, you won't see me. Then you will see me."*

The afternoon passed slowly. Sarah played in little bursts, but her thoughts kept returning to her broken doll and the promise her mother had made. Time seemed to stretch endlessly.

Hours later, Sarah sat quietly on the couch, gently brushing her doll's hair, her small fingers moving with care.

"Hey," her sister Penny called from across the room, "I thought the pony stepped on your dolly."

"He did," Sarah replied proudly, "but Mom gave her a new arm."

"Let me see," Penny said, reaching for the doll.

"No!" Sarah protested, pulling the doll closer to her chest. "You can't see!"

A struggle broke out as Penny tugged at the doll.

"That's my doll!" Penny shouted, frustration rising. "You didn't ask me!" Penny yelled, pulling at the doll's new arm.

"No!" Sarah cried again, her voice full of panic and fear.

With one last sharp pull, the doll's arm snapped off again. Sarah's heart clenched, tears springing back as she stared at the now-broken doll.

Just then, a delicate butterfly with sparkling wings drifted into the room, its colors glinting as it danced gracefully. Both girls froze, their eyes locked on the tiny, glowing creature.

The butterfly hovered fleetingly, then gently landed on the doll's broken arm, as if offering comfort. Sarah's tears slowed, her breathing calm as she watched, mesmerized. Penny, too, paused, her anger fading as awe took its place.

For a quiet moment, the butterfly's fragile fluttering seemed to fill the room with something unspoken: a reminder of gentleness and the need for care. Penny's grip loosened, and she let go of the doll's arm, her voice softer now.

"Maybe we can fix her together," she suggested with quiet remorse.

Sarah nodded, her heart lifting.

"Okay," she whispered, still watching as the butterfly lifted off, circling once before gliding out the window, leaving behind a trail of quiet hope and peace.

Chapter 10: The Shining Path

Moments later, a hush settled over everything, as if the world held its breath. Then her uncle's soft and clear voice drifted to her like a breeze through an open window.

"You are not asleep. It is a dream, but you're not dreaming," he whispered gently.

Before Sarah could answer, the world around her lifted and dissolved. Suddenly, she was somewhere else entirely, a place that felt far beyond time. She was three again, lying in her small bed, when an angel appeared, glowing softly, and lifted her high above, carrying her straight to heaven.

In awe, Sarah gazed around her, eyes wide as wonder entered her heart. Spotting Jesus, she moved closer and asked shyly, "Did I do good things? Do you watch me?"

Jesus smiled, his eyes warm and kind.

"Precious child, you I have chosen. Yes, I have always watched you, and I will continue to watch you."

Sarah's heart swelled with happiness.

"God, can I stay here forever and ever? This place is so beautiful and peaceful," she whispered, her voice full of longing as she stared at the endless blue sky dotted with soft, white clouds.

"You will, my child," a gentle voice answered, wrapping around her like a warm hug on a chilly day.

Sarah's eyes shimmered with hope.

"Can my mommy and daddy come too?" she asked, her voice small but full of yearning.

"Everyone you love will be here," the voice replied, reassuring and kind.

Sarah closed her eyes with a soft sigh, picturing a place where everyone she loved was safe and joyful.

"Will a big tree be in our backyard like the big one in my front yard?" she asked hopefully.

"And many more," the voice promised, its tone soothing.

A deep sense of peace wrapped around Sarah.

"I love you, God," she whispered, her words full of quiet devotion.

When she opened her eyes again, everything had transformed. The colors were brighter and richer. The air felt crisp and new. Birds sang in perfect harmony, their songs weaving together like a joyful chorus. Leaves swayed gently in the breeze, their movement almost musical. Every blade of grass and every flower seemed to shine with vibrant life.

Sarah breathed deeply, savoring the clean, fresh air. She could hear the soft buzz of bees nearby and the bubbling of a stream in the distance, its gentle flow adding to the calm. Sunlight filtered through the trees, forming playful patterns of shadow and light, while the sweet scent of blooming flowers mingled with the earthy smell of the forest floor.

Jesus turned to her, his eyes bright with joy.

"These are elders. Can you count this many?" he asked, his eyes twinkling.

Sarah straightened proudly.

"Yes, I can count to ten!" she said confidently.

Jesus smiled warmly.

"Okay, you count ten, and I will count the other four and ten."

The peaceful sounds of birdsong and rustling leaves wrapped around them as they counted together, making everything feel serene and safe.

Jesus's voice softened, full of love. "Do you know how much I love you?" he asked, watching her closely.

Sarah nodded, her voice certain. "Yes, I really know. You died for my sins, but you're not dead because you're standin' right there!"

A golden glow seemed to brighten the air around them, and the soft sounds of nature blended seamlessly with their words.

Jesus laughed, a sound as gentle and refreshing as a light rain. He lifted Sarah and set her on a large, sturdy chair.

"How do you know?" he asked, smiling with curiosity.

Sarah beamed.

"Because I know a lot of important information, and you told me," she said proudly.

Jesus's eyes softened.

"There are three things you must do for me," he continued, his voice filled with care. "First, believe in the power in me. I will be with you always."

Sarah felt her heart swell with faith, her eyes shining.

"Another, what I give to you, you will keep forever, and until."

Curiosity flashed across her face, but she nodded eagerly.

"And again, when you grow big, you will write of what was in a little book chosen. Will you do these things for me?"

"Yes, I will," Sarah promised, trying to sound as grown-up as possible.

Jesus's smile grew, and the space around them seemed to pulse with gentle energy.

"Remember, I will always be with you."

The peaceful sounds of birds and leaves stirred the air, keeping the moment calm. Sarah felt a powerful sense of purpose settle deep inside her.

The golden light glowed brighter, wrapping her in its warmth.

"I will do anything forever. I promise," she said with quiet determination.

Jesus gently lifted her down from the chair, placing his hands on her head. In that instant, brilliant colors poured from her, swirling and glowing.

She giggled, spinning around as the magical light danced and twinkled around her.

"Oh, look at me! I am so beautiful!"

Jesus laughed softly.

"Follow me," he said.

Sarah followed closely, her heart full of joy. Everything around her seemed to glisten with life. She felt as though she could see straight into her soul, each step painting a vivid picture in her mind. The sounds of rustling leaves, cheerful birds, and the babbling brook wove together like a perfect melody. The warm, golden light bathed everything, enveloping the scene in quiet beauty.

Her laughter rang out, mingling with the peaceful sounds of the forest. This sacred moment, with all its colors, music, and deep peace, imprinted itself on her heart, a memory she knew would last forever.

Chapter 11: The Singing Gardens

Sarah's laughter faded into a quiet stillness as the forest around her began to change. The golden light softened, folding into mist, and the melody of birdsong gave way to silence. It was as if time itself had paused, waiting.

Sarah blinked.

Her senses reeled. The world around her transitioned.

She was no longer following Jesus through the glistening woods; instead, she felt herself drifting, floating backward through memory, deeper into a place that was both familiar and strange.

She recognized it not with her eyes, but with her heart. A place made of old questions, half-remembered dreams, and things left unsaid.

"The truth is in the tree of life," Sarah heard her uncle gently say as she floated into a place of yesterday, where tomorrow never came and today never was.

The words echoed softly as the scene around her changed. The light dimmed, cooler now, and the warmth of the forest gave way to the faint chill of an early morning long ago. She was smaller, her legs dangled above the floor, and her hands gripped the end of a blanket. A memory was unfolding, vivid and alive.

She turned and saw her sister, Penny, now eight, while Sarah was six. Penny appeared to have wet hair clinging to her cheeks, wrapped in a towel, and shivering.

"Why did they put you in the river?" Sarah asked her with concern.

"That's holy water," Penny explained. "You have to be baptized if you want to go to heaven."

"That water ain't holy water; it's the river," Sarah replied.

"I know it's the river," Penny insisted, "but they prayed and made the water holy. If you don't get into the river, you will see all the monsters in heaven. I won't see the monsters because I was washed clean." There was a note of pride in her voice. "Now, go away and stop bothering me!" she added, turning away and pulling the towel more tightly around her.

My sister Penny was baptized today; she is pure, and I'm not. Sarah sat on her bed, thinking.

A wave of sadness crept over her, an aching feeling of being unworthy.

"God," she prayed in a hushed manner, "you know I always try to be clean." Tears welled in her eyes. "I don't want to see the monsters in heaven. I want to be clean like my sister, but do I have to get in the water? Jesus, do you hear me? I love you and know you died for my sins."

She sobbed quietly, her shoulders trembling. "Please don't show me the monsters in heaven." Worn out, she slipped into sleep, her sister's image, cleansed and radiant, lingering in her thoughts.

An angel appeared beside her. He said, "You can call me Michael. There are no monsters in heaven, and I will show you!" His voice was gentle, his smile kind.

They rose together on a cloud softer than anything she had known, ascending higher until a breathtaking vision unfolded; not a castle, but a vast, wondrous city. The very air sparkled, filled with a warmth that eased all fear.

They neared a magnificent gate, three gates, in fact; each one luminous, like immense pearls glowing with light.

"Oh, Michael, look!" Sarah exclaimed.

Figures of extraordinary beauty stood beside the gates. Their wings, translucent and gleaming like opals, caught the celestial light.

Their serene faces radiated pure love and peace.

"Yes, Sarah," Michael replied, his tone reverent. "They are the gatekeepers, welcoming us home."

A thrill ran through her. Beyond the gates, the city unfolded: towering crystal spires reached toward the heavens, catching light and scattering it in brilliant patterns. Endless gardens bloomed in radiant colors, every petal glowing with life. A harmony of voices wove through the air, creating a music that stirred the soul.

"Can you count them for me?" Michael asked.

"One! Two! Three!" Sarah counted with delight.

"Very good!" he said.

"I can even count to thirty, but sometimes I get mixed up on fourteen and fifteen," she confessed.

"Sarah, would you like to count all the angels? Do not worry. There are not too many here to count. You will not be confused," Michael assured her.

"Okay, but I already counted these three," she said, pointing skyward.

"Those are just the beginning."

"There is more waiting for you to count them," Michael said, smiling at her eagerness.

Together, they glided through the radiant city. Soon, they reached an immense library, its shelves lined with books that pulsed with a quiet brilliance.

"Look, Michael!" Sarah pointed at an enormous volume. "Can we read that one?"

Michael nodded. "Of course, Sarah. Every book in this library holds knowledge of the universe. Choose any you like."

As she reached out, a soft melody glided through the air. The book's pages flickered with images and tales as they ventured further into the city.

Structures—if they could be called that—glistened with shifting, iridescent hues, as if they breathed and adapted to those who dwelled inside.

"Look, Michael!" Sarah gasped, pointing ahead.

A sweeping expanse of color opened before them; a garden unlike any other. Blues like sapphires, greens rich as emeralds, fiery oranges, and golden hues like sunsets stretched across the horizon. Each flower pulsed with vibrant life, and the breeze carried a cascade of delicate, celestial melodies.

"Hmm. Those are the Singing Gardens," Michael said with wonder. "Each flower's song is a different melody, and together they create a symphony of joy."

They moved onward, arriving at a broad, crystalline river. Its waters were so clear that Sarah could see the riverbed, where radiant, multicolored fish darted playfully.

"This is the River of Life," Michael told her. "Its water brings eternal life and healing to all who drink from it."

Sarah dipped her hand into the current and felt a tingling warmth, as though it carried the energy of creation itself.

"It's so refreshing," she said, beaming.

They floated on, passing through places where angels gathered. The gentle rustle of wings mingled with soft, chiming sounds. The market buzzed, not like the ones on Earth, but with a sense of delight and quiet purpose. Sarah tilted her head, watching as angels crafted toys or perhaps shared the joy of their beautiful creations. Some shaped light into intricate forms; others flipped through books that seemed to hold the secrets of the stars.

"Everything here is perfect," she whispered, eyes wide in wonder.

Michael nodded. "And it will always be."

As their laughter faded into the soft whirr of heaven, the sky began to change. The sun dipped low, painting the city in warm pinks and golden hues. A hush settled over the scene like a blanket of peace. Sarah breathed it in, a calm she had never known settling deep inside her. She glanced at Michael and, in his eyes, saw the gentle affection of a friend who had always been near.

"I love it here, Michael," she said softly.

Michael smiled. "And I love you being here, Sarah. Hold my hand, and I will show you."

She slipped her hand into his, and they stepped forward.

"Four, five, six!" Sarah counted.

Another step. "Seven, eight, nine!"

Then one more. "Ten, eleven, twelve! I can't count what's next," she said with a sheepish smile.

"That's because I told you, you will not be confused. We are back to where we started. So, how many angels did you count?" Michael asked, his eyes warm with pride.

"Twelve!" Sarah declared.

"Then so it is!" Michael laughed gently.

"Wow!" Sarah giggled. "Look at that house over there; it's so large and beautiful. You probably need a lot of money to have a house like that," she said, marveling at its vibrant colors. "I wish my family could live in a house like that. I bet we would each have our own bedroom. It's so big. Look at all those colors."

"These are true colors," Michael replied. "Would you like to go inside?"

"Should I take off my filthy shoes?" Sarah asked, glancing down at her dusty feet.

"Can you crawl through the eye of a needle?" he asked.

"Why do you ask me a funny thing like that?" she responded.

"I choose to guide you," Michael said. "Do you understand what that means?"

"I sure do," Sarah answered. "I know a lot of important information."

They walked a few more steps before Michael pointed ahead. "Look! There are no monsters here."

Sarah looked around. The light around them was radiant, but not harsh. She could still see everything clearly.

As she took in her surroundings, she noticed the polished surface beneath their feet.

"Wow! My mommy would really, really like these floors. They are so shiny," Sarah said, bending to touch them. The surface was smooth, like glass beneath her fingers. "My brothers drag me on a blanket to polish our floors at our house. How do you get such a beautiful shine?"

Her eyes turned to the walls. "And these walls, how did you make these pretty colors?" she asked, admiring the richly painted surfaces. "Can I stay forever?"

Sarah looked up at Michael.

"Yes, you can stay here forever and ever more, but not yet. We are not ready for you yet. I will show you again when the time comes."

"Believe what I say, and you will know the way," she heard.

"Oh, that rhymes!"

She giggled and began to sing, *"Believe what I say, and you will know the way.* Can I keep it? Can I sing it when I play hopscotch with my sister?"

They began to sing together and hop like they were playing hopscotch.

"Believe what I say." With a leap from both feet, they continued, *"And I will know the way."* Sarah heard Michael giggle.

They hopped on one foot in sync. *"And I will show you again, Believe..."*

As their playful game ended, Michael pointed to a small cloud, about the size of a bed pillow.

"Look inside this cloud. What do you see?" he asked.

"I see music," Sarah said.

"You can see music?" Michael asked, laughing.

"What does music look like?"

"Why do you ask me such a simple question? Look in there, you can see it too," she insisted.

"I know what I see. I was just wondering what your eyes may see. Being the eyes of a child, you may see things differently than I do."

"Oh well then! Do you see that sound right there?" Sarah asked, pointing toward a soft chime in the little cloud.

Michael looked closely. "You mean that little chiming sound?"

"Yeah. That sound—you're so silly, Michael, that's the only sound there is. Of course, I mean the chiming sound," she said with playful exasperation.

"Okay. Yes, I see it," he said.

"Well! What does it look like?" she asked.

"Okay.. enough for now," Michael said, "we will come back to this a little later. There is more I want you to see."

He pointed to another small cloud. "Look in this cloud and tell me what you see."

Sarah leaned in and peered closely. "Ah, look!" she laughed with excitement.

"What do you see?" Michael asked.

"Wow, look!" Sarah exclaimed, her eyes wide. "I see a little boy on top of the barn. He's all lit up with pretty lights!"

"The Rainbow Lights!" Michael said with excitement. "They do glow!"

"Where did he get all those colors from?" Sarah asked in wonder. "I think he's very happy. I bet I know what he's thinking. I bet he thinks he can fly."

"He is filled with the Holy Spirit," Michael said, his voice suddenly solemn.

As Sarah watched, the boy in the cloud suddenly jumped and fell.

She gasped. "Why doesn't he get up? Is he dead?"

Instantly, two angels appeared; one at the boy's head, one at his feet. Sarah's tears came quickly.

"Why did the angels let him fall?" she cried.

"Why do you cry, child?" Michael asked gently. "Look closer."

Still crying, Sarah leaned in again. Despite the brightness of the light, she could see. She focused, and her eyes widened.

"Oh, look!" she exclaimed. "Two little white baby birds, as doves, pick up the boy and stand him on his feet!"

Her sobbing stopped as she watched the doves lift him. Peace returned to her face.

"You call him Bobby," Michael said.

"Bobby? My biggest brother in the entire world?" Sarah asked, recalling a story her mother once told them. Bobby had climbed onto the barn roof and fallen, but he was okay.

"The river is like bread and wine," a voice said. "One lives—not without the other."

"Do you know who is talking to you?" Michael asked.

"Of course I know—it's Jesus, you silly Michael!" Sarah replied with certainty.

"Do you know what he is saying to you?" Michael asked again.

"Of course, *I know*," Sarah answered proudly. "I know important information because Jesus gave me bread with a book inside."

Everything seemed to pause for a heartbeat, then change again.

Suddenly, Sarah felt warmth in her hand; her uncle was holding it. A deep, resonant sound surrounded them. Thousands of souls were singing. Though they chanted in many tongues, every voice carried the same message, vibrating through every atom of Sarah's being.

"Al---Le---Lu' ---IA!" they chanted repeatedly.

As their voices rose, Sarah became aware of something unusual. She wasn't moving forward in time; she was floating through yesterday, walking away from tomorrow, while today remained just out of reach. It was as though she were traveling through a vast telescope; broad at the base, narrowing into a distant light point.

At the far end, a pure and radiant amber glow shone. She reached toward it, longing to be filled with the overwhelming love that radiated from within. She ached for the light. Around her, countless souls reached, too, drawn to its pull. She could see them. She could hear them.

"Al---Le--- Lu' ---IA!" they chanted in perfect unison.

Sarah could feel the souls beside her. Each one was watching, listening, knowing. She sensed an unbreakable bond between them, like threads in a great tapestry, ancient and sacred. Her hands brushed against its invisible weave, and with every touch, stories and memories whispered to her. Then, without warning, a raw scream tore from her lips, a cry not of pain, but of recognition. Her soul had found its voice and thundered across the eternal fabric of creation.

"I know you!" she cried, her words shaking the colors of the tapestry, causing them to swirl and transition.

The souls stirred. Their energy rose, mingling with hers. A pulse of power surged through her, and she understood: she was not alone.

She touched them, saw everything, felt everything. Past and future collided, and she knew them all.

Her soul screamed again, and this time, every soul heard.

"I know you!"

Her uncle squeezed her hand gently. "Through adherence, I share my light, and you shall see."

And she did.

Sarah saw music, literal, shimmering music. She saw her family stretching back generations. The path widened before her. Multitudes of souls walked with her, all desperate to reach the light. Many reached out to embrace her, but they could not stop. The pull of the light was too strong, too urgent.

Voices filled the air, clashing in a confused chorus of languages: Hebrew, German, Irish, French, Native tongues, and many more. They cried out together, unintelligible yet unified in longing. Amid the chaos, Sarah saw something, in fact, heard something: the music of her generation's souls.

Then, she was stumbling, lost in a scorching desert. Her vision blurred with thirst. Sand moved under her feet. A weak rustling caught her attention, and she turned to find a mirage forming in the heat.

As she neared, the image transformed: a lush oasis rising from the barren earth. Palm trees swayed gently, and a clear stream sparkled under the sun. Her name echoed softly in the air, spoken by a kind voice. A fragile hope bloomed in her chest. The light, once so far, seemed to draw closer.

But the voices in her mind grew louder, clamoring, contradicting, pulling her apart.

She staggered, with every step feeling heavier than the last. The burning sand scorched her feet, and her thirst clawed at her insides. She was exhausted and nearly broken, but moved forward, desperate for the promise hidden in the oasis.

The voices surrounded her, a cacophony of pleading tongues. She wanted to reach the light, but the chaos made it nearly impossible to think, let alone move.

Her body cried out. Her skin burned. Her head throbbed. Her lips were cracked with dryness. There was no strength left to speak. She couldn't even summon the breath to pray aloud.

But her soul cried silently.

"God, do you hear me? Please give me water; I'm so thirsty," Sarah thought as loudly as she could.

Her hand slipped from her uncle's grasp as she clutched her ears, trying to block the relentless noise. Her knees buckled. She collapsed into the searing sand.

She couldn't walk any farther. She couldn't go on.

The voices moved closer.

And then, her uncle knelt beside her and gently placed both hands over her eyes.

Chapter 12: The Eternal Path

A sound rose, not from the outside, but from within. A harmonious symphony erupted from unseen beings, as a chorus of voices wove together in perfect celestial harmony. Every language blended seamlessly into one great chime, resonant, unified, and vast.

Sarah felt it immediately.

A surge of power pulsed through her as a wave of undivided love swept over her soul, flooding every part of her. The unity of sound became an order, clear, resounding, absolute. As if summoned into sacred stillness, the countless voices ceased their chatter.

People were saying, "Hallelujah!"

Sarah looked around and saw her friends. They smiled at her, and she heard the soft tinkle of little bells.

Her uncle's voice grounded her: "This is real."

A glow of happiness spread within her. She felt small, but not insignificant. She felt safe. She felt like she had come home.

Sarah didn't speak. She wrote what she heard:

"I that speak unto thee am He.
Oh, faithless generation, do you need a sign?
Take up that household and follow me.
Ask what I shall give you.
Who claims this divided generation?
Are the little ones divided?
And when the little ones reach out for fulfillment,
Do you speak in parables that they cannot understand?
For you say tomorrow, and tomorrow you say never comes.
Now is the accepted time.
The path to follow is narrow; therefore, why do you take the
wide?
Who claims this faithless generation?
Now is the accepted time, and every eye shall see."

Suddenly, time shifted again, accelerating, bending forward.

Far off, the harmonious chiming rang in perfect unity. A barely audible hum began to rise, a sound that didn't come from around her, but from her soul. It glowed softly like an amber light.

She felt herself pulled forward, irresistibly, drawn into a blind and welcoming brilliance. Peace flooded her.

And then, she was no longer where she had been.

She had entered another realm entirely.

Before her stretched a breathtaking garden, a creation beyond imagination, it radiated beauty and peace in equal measure. Every flower shone with its light, its forms intricate and otherworldly.

Each bloom reflected light like stained glass, changing hues across the sky-like canopy above. The air was alive with music, a melody that wrapped around her like a warm wind. A soft blue glow blanketed the space, soothing and serene.

Sarah reached toward a petal, and as she did, a gentle breeze carried the sweet, exotic scent of the flowers to her. It filled her lungs with vitality. With every breath, she felt renewed, as though each cell in her body had awakened. She knew it then, without question, this was home.

A powerful energy rose within her, as if she were plugged into the source of all being. She felt herself expand, limitless. Capable of leading, of building, of simply existing as she was meant to.

Music filled the garden, weaving through every corner of her soul, bathing her in unconditional love. Her very atoms responded, resonating with divine harmony.

A gasp escaped her lips, not from surprise, but from wonder.

She could breathe fully here. Joy spilled from within her. She felt lighter than air, lifted by an invisible force, her spirit soaring across the garden. At that moment, she saw herself clearly, without fear or limits.

A cocoon of soft, translucent warmth wrapped around her like an embrace, protective yet gentle. She looked up. A crystalline star hung above her, glowing with a pure, white brilliance. Its light poured across the garden, illuminating every shade and surface with gentle pastel blue.

Within this light, vibrant colors began to bloom: lush apple trees heavy with crimson fruit, radiant flowers of every hue, blossoming in impossible combinations. The scene felt like paradise reborn. From the corner of her vision, a delicate butterfly appeared with iridescent and aglow wings. It fluttered gracefully, its path weaving gently through the luminous flowers. Sarah watched it, enchanted. Its soft, blue-tinged wings caught the light as if made of glass and light.

The butterfly settled softly on one of the blossoms. Its small presence felt like an invitation, a message just for her. As it rested, Sarah felt an even deeper connection to the garden around her. With the butterfly as her silent guide, she sensed the garden was alive with meaning. Every detail mattered. Every moment was a miracle.

Then, her uncle appeared once again, suddenly, yet peacefully. He stood within the cocoon with her, familiar and yet transformed.

Beside him, a vision of light unfolded: a rich, deep blue illuminated by a golden ring that hovered just above it. As the blue deepened and shifted, the golden halo moved with it, connected by some sacred law.

Her uncle reached out and gently touched the cocoon that surrounded her.

Curious, Sarah looked through its veil and saw something just beyond: a head of golden-brown hair resting beneath an expanse of vibrant blue. The longer she looked, the more intense the blue became, expanding, deepening, inviting her into its mystery.

She didn't want to leave.

She wanted this moment—this place—to stretch on forever.

The blue light passed through the cocoon and flooded her senses. She felt it enter her fully. Then came a rich and eternal voice.

"Do you know how much I love you?"

The words echoed again. And again. A rhythm in her chest, in her bones, in her breath. The question became everything.

Sarah's vision was filled with faces: her children, her husband, her parents, her siblings… and even her beloved pets. And then, she saw music.

Each soul was a canvas for love's endless message, spoken through the song of all things. It was a love older than the stars, stretching beyond time, cradling her in its certainty.

She was four years old and stood in the kitchen doorway, small and quiet. Her mommy and Daddy were talking.

Something in their voices caught her attention, a change.

"The duck died," Daddy said, voice low and heavy.

Her mommy nodded. Her eyes filled with a sadness Sarah didn't understand.

The stillness in the room was thick, the impact of those few words sinking into Sarah's small chest.

"He swallowed a bee, and he died."

Outside, the world spun in chaos. Panic blurred her vision as the turkey loomed, a monstrous shadow chasing her. It's thunder gobbled like a drumbeat in her ears. Somewhere nearby, something struck the ground with a sharp crack, and her father's angry voice cut through the noise like lightning.

Sarah ran.

In the pen, she found the still and lifeless Quacker. His head, cool in her tiny hands, made her cry. Her tears were quiet, her sorrow deeper than words.

"Do you know how much I love you, Quacker?" she whispered inside, holding tightly.

But Daddy's voice broke into her silence.

"Sunday dinner," he said, flat and final.

She could still see him carrying Quacker toward the cold, concrete slab. That image, etched into her heart, became a seed of fear buried deep inside her. Her mother had held her close that day, promising they wouldn't eat him, but Sarah could never quite believe it.

And then came the nightmares, swarms of them, like angry bees. She'd wake soaked in sweat, heart racing, trapped in fear. The bees were always there, chasing her.

"Jesus help me! The bees are chasing me! Please save me!" Sarah prayed.

And then, stillness. A gentle hand. A soothing voice.

WHAT DO YOU SEE?

"Hold out that leg," Daddy said, dabbing balm onto her stinging skin.

And again, she heard the whisper:

"I work the works of him that sent me, even in your sleep."

Light bloomed. Sarah opened her eyes. The world shimmered differently. A new promise had taken root. A path had formed. She looked deeper into the blue, and it opened before her.

She was four again.

She clung tightly to her mother's leg. "Mommy, I don't want a shot!" she begged.

"It won't hurt," her mother assured her, gently leading her out the door.

The walk uptown was long for such small legs. Exhaustion tugged at Sarah, and her nerves grew heavier with every step.

When the bus arrived, they boarded. The short ride into town echoed with Sarah's sobs. Her younger brother, Eddie, just three years old, reached for her hand.

"It'll only hurt for a little while, Sarah. Then it'll be over," he said kindly.

They sat on stiff chairs at the health department among other anxious children. The room was full of sniffles and uneasy whispers. Eddie's hand stayed wrapped around hers. Though he was scared too, he masked it because he was a boy, and boys were supposed to be brave. Eddie never showed fear. At least, not out loud.

Then the nurse called their names. Eddie, Sarah, and their sister Kathy, five years old, stood to go inside. Their mother held baby Toby, bouncing him softly in her arms.

Kathy went first.

"No! You said it would only hurt for a second—and it hurt bad!" she shrieked.

Sarah gasped. "Oh no," she cried. "I don't want to get a shot! I don't want to get a shot!"

Their mother passed baby Toby to a nurse and lifted Sarah into her arms. Eddie had just gotten his shot and ran over, trying to calm her.

"Oh, Sarah, it didn't hurt. I just got mine. It only took a second. Don't worry," he reassured.

The nurse gave Toby his shot, and he cried briefly before being comforted with a lollipop.

Sarah bit down on her thumb, bracing herself, as the needle approached. "I don't want to get a shot!" she yelled again.

Then—a flutter of color.

A delicate butterfly with shimmering, iridescent wings floated into the room. It moved with grace, circling gently above her. Sarah's eyes locked onto it, mesmerized. Her fear faded as the butterfly landed softly on her shoulder. Its quiet presence brought calm. She held her breath, watching it. Just as the nurse finished, the butterfly lifted off and flew around the room again, leaving a sense of peace.

"Why are you screaming? You already got the shot," her mother said.

"I did? Oh—it didn't even hurt!" Sarah exclaimed in marvel.

The butterfly had made all the difference. She smiled, brave now, and accepted her lollipop with pride.

Then, just as suddenly, the scene changed.

Sarah was back in Ms. McGee's classroom. The air was warm and dry, the faint scent of chalk and old wood clinging to the walls. That day, they learned about trees.

Ms. McGee stood at the front, holding a small, green sapling.

"This is yours to care for," she said.

Each student was given a tree, a symbol of growth and responsibility. Sarah imagined hers growing tall, sheltering birds, and shading picnic blankets. Ms. McGee explained the basics: sunlight, soil, and space.

Sarah listened closely, imagining her tree reaching the sky. "Maybe I could build a treehouse!" she exclaimed. "But what if my brother wants to plant his tree nearby?"

She raised her hand.

Ms. McGee smiled warmly. "That's fine, Sarah. Trees like company."

The thought thrilled her. Her tree. Her duty. A living piece of the world in her care.

"Can I take care of his tree too?" she asked.

"If he wants your help, that's fine," Ms. McGee replied. "But the tree belongs to him."

The class fell into thoughtful silence. A shared sense of wonder filled the room, and everyone cradled their own little sapling of hope.

The bell rang. It was time to choose.

But just as excitement sparked across the classroom, Sarah felt her uncle's hands on her shoulders.

"Write this down," he said urgently.

She picked up her pencil. The words spilled from her soul as if etched in fire:

"What does this generation see? Are you lost? I promised clarity.

Why don't you ask me? I will show you.

Who owns this divided world?

Are our children broken?

Is there no solid ground to stand upon?

Does no one claim this lost generation?

God is the supreme leader, and his plan is to be fulfilled.

He called upon his chosen people to follow his guidance.

This is his beloved son; listen to me!

God desires a new way of life, free from the burdens of the past.

He seeks those who will establish new foundations for the generation to grow.

Those who embrace this new path must protect the innocence of the young and lead them toward a brighter future.

To follow God's word, you must abandon the ways of this generation and embrace a new, yet ancient, way of life.

Those who resist this change will be left behind.

God's chosen people will hear his voice and follow him, united in purpose and strength.

This generation lacks the unity and strength to build a new world.

It is time for a new beginning, led by those who answer God's call.

So, how many did you count...? As oneness, thine eye be full.

Believe what I say, and you will know the way.

Those who believe will believe. Those who don't believe will believe."

The words echoed in her mind like thunder across a mountain range.

"What do you see?" her uncle asked.

"Look into the light, and you will see. Through the light, you will hear."

Sarah hesitated.

Slowly, she lifted her gaze.

A crystal ball hovered before her, pulsing with mesmerizing energy. A radiant blue beam spiraled upward from its core, moving in rhythm like a living current. As she looked deeper, the world began to dissolve around her, replaced by a cascade of colors and shapes, moving in a kaleidoscopic rhythm.

And then she saw: a vision.

With his face shining, her little brother bathed in a joyful light.

"You're such a special little brother," a voice whispered, gentle and full of love. *"You're my very bestest friend, and I love you."*

The vision transitioned.

Now she saw a quaint little house nestled among blooming flowers. A voice continued, filled with hope and certainty:

"We are going to buy our mom a new house. It is going to have real water, and we can drink the water."

And Sarah could hear.

Laughter echoed softly. The murmur of a stream rolled in the background. Birds chirped in the distance, creating a melody of joy and promise. It was the sound of a future full of love, of life overflowing with peace.

"As oneness, thine eye be full. This little one is my chosen one. He that has ears to hear, let him hear."

Suddenly, she was far from home.

The sun blazed above a dusty road, its heat pressing like a heavy blanket. Her little brother stood nearby, face flushed red, raising his hand to knock on an old wooden door.

She heard her father's voice from the backyard:

"Watch me, Daddy, watch me! Are you still watching me?"

She saw herself surrounded by family, learning to draw.

"Draw your house like this," they told her gently.

She followed their guidance, the lines forming in her mind before they touched the page: simple shapes, bright colors, her home, alive in memory and imagination. And then she heard it: a soft and loving voice, full of reverence:

"You just glow in the dark."

It continued, *"As oneness thine eye be full...*
You believe in me; I believe in you, too.
The love you give me is within you, and I am within you also.

You follow me. I will follow you also.

You will not see me for a little while, but then you will see me.

I am with you, and I am with you always."

"Fathers, take up your household and follow me.

Do the fathers know not the fathers? Do the sons know not the

sons?

Do the mothers know, not the mothers? Do the daughters know,

not the daughters?

Does the family know not their family?

As the father knows me, even so, I know the father.

Are your doors locked?"

"Truly, I say to you, I am the door, and I am the key.

You will not know at what time I will come.

Are you ready? What do you see?

You ask what else I can give to you.

Now is the accepted time, and every eye shall see."

"First, you take one step on one foot. Pick up your

household and follow me.

Now, you take one step on both feet. Lay claim to that

household and follow me.

Now is the accepted time. Lay claim to this divided generation.

Follow me, and I will guide you.

You follow with me; I follow with you too.

The father knows me; even so, I know the father, for the father
and I are as one."

   "He that has the ears to hear, let him hear.

He that has the eyes to see, let him see.

Can you count them for me? Would you like to count all of them?

You won't have to count so many that you will be confused.

Every eye shall see."

   The message repeated—again and again—until it became part of her.

   Sarah traveled to a place of Until. It was a realm outside of time, where there was no ticking clock but all the time in the world. A place, deep within her soul, where her eye took a picture, one that would never fade.

   "What do you see?" her uncle asked.

   He stood next to a tiny cloud, one hand resting on its delicate form, the other extended toward her.

   "What do you see?" Michael echoed, taking her hand gently.

   He tilted his head, playful but curious.

   "Did you say you can see music? What does music look like?" he asked as Sarah peered into the cloud.

   "Yes, I see it," she replied.

"Well! What does it look like?" Michael asked again, curiosity blooming in his voice.

And she saw again and heard...

"Watch me, Daddy, watch me." A little girl's voice, her own, so clear. "It's so big and beautiful..." A gasp escaped her lips, unbidden.

The colors weren't just bright; they were a mix of shock and revelation. Brighter, impossibly brighter, than anything she could ever recall seeing.

"I bet we could each have our own bedroom," she'd declared, with a childish certainty.

Then another voice, sharp with joy, broke through the shimmering fragments of time. As a rush of voices sounded, she heard another voice.

"She's here! You're home!" It was her sister.

"Come on, follow me, you'll see!"

Her family's voices were a chorus now, overlapping, insistent, and pulling her forward through the mists of time. It was as though a dam had broken, and the torrent of what was, of what she'd loved and lost and forgotten, surged back, demanding to be seen and to be felt.

With hands reaching and laughter echoing, they were all coming back, tumbling over each other like a kaleidoscope of moments she hadn't known she'd lost.

"Where are you all going?"

"Follow me, you'll see."

"Do you need a sign or something? It's a secret."

"I know what you're getting for your birthday."

"Let me give it to her."

The world exploded in a riot of hues, each one singing, vibrant, and impossibly real. Colors pulsed around her, radiant and alive, a breathtaking spectacle. Beneath it all, a gentle yet immense melody began to swell, wrapping around her like a comforting embrace. Then, a hushed whisper, close to her ear.

"Look! She's playing with her eyes closed," a voice murmured, tinged with awe. Another voice, softer but firm, corrected,

"She's not practicing! She's playing!" countered by a frustrated, "She's not *practicing* 'Do You Hear What I Hear?' She's *playing*— **I Can't Hear!**"

The fragments swirled, vivid and immediate, each snippet of sound and color a key unlocking a forgotten chamber within her mind.

"I can feel…" Sarah breathed, her voice thick with a dawning understanding. "I don't need to see to hear."

It was a revelation, a truth blooming within her. Each note of the swelling music materialized as a vibrant drop of color, one melting seamlessly into the next, a liquid cascade of pure sensation. It wasn't just sound; it was a living melody, painting itself across the canvas of her senses, visible in a way sight alone could never capture. She saw the music, felt its vibrations resonate deep within her, filling every space. Each note pulsed with an undeniable warmth, a layer of pure love intertwined with unwavering truth, singing directly to the very core of her being.

A desperate plea escaped her lips. "Please, can I stay here now? Please?"

Her uncle's hands, gentle yet firm, enclosed hers. "Through adherence, I shine my light, and you will see," he said, his voice resonating with a profound certainty. "You cannot stay here now. We are not ready for you yet."

Michael reached forward, his hands moving through the transparent covering of one of the enclosed forms. Sarah's uncle did the same.

Sarah followed, placing her hand on the form. In a flash, she was there, standing before her as the color amber enveloped her. It was vivid, golden, and alive.

"I belong here. I came from here!" Sarah cried from somewhere deep inside.

The music of her soul twirled around her, lifting her in its embrace. She turned, eyes wide with wonder.

"Look at all these beautiful colors," she thought to Michael, overcome by the magnificence surrounding her.

Her uncle touched her hand gently.

"Would you like to go inside?" he asked.

A soft green light wrapped around her like a blanket. Two enormous emerald wings folded inward, shielding her in warmth and safety.

"And every eye shall see," her uncle whispered, giggling softly.

And just like that, they were inside. Peace took over her. Her heart ached, not with fear, but with longing.

"But why can't I stay here?" Sarah asked, her voice trembling.

Her uncle exhaled slowly, sadness in his eyes.

"This is a place of transition—a space between life and what comes next. It's not a permanent home."

Sarah gazed around the gleaming chamber, where countless reflections of herself sparkled like light on water.

"I don't want to leave," she whispered.

Her uncle knelt beside her.

"I know, Sarah. Saying goodbye to this place is hard. But there's more waiting for you." He squeezed her hand, steadying her.

"Remember—you're never alone. I'll always be with you. Watching."

Tears welled in her eyes, but she nodded. They turned and walked away together. Sarah glanced back once more. She knew she would never forget this place, or the peace it brought. But her journey wasn't finished. Not yet.

As they stepped forward, the scene around her transformed again.

Sarah stood in the courtyard of a castle unlike any she had ever imagined. Its walls shimmered with translucent marble, its towers stretching endlessly into the sky.

Surrounding the castle were vibrant gardens, blossoming with every flower she could name and some she couldn't. Their perfume drifted in the breeze, and birdsong filled the air. She breathed in deeply. The peace returned, anchoring her. Her uncle smiled.

"This is your new home," he said.

Chapter 13: The Journey Begins

Sarah felt the breeze carry the scent of blossoms through the garden. Her eyes widened in amazement. She had never seen a place so beautiful. Every step toward the castle brought her growing excitement; an inner knowing that her journey was far from over.

They slowly approached the gates.

"Look closely," her uncle said.

Sarah turned and glanced to the side and saw her father walking slowly down a long, golden staircase that shone in the center of the room. In his hands, he held something precious.

"What do you see?" her uncle asked.

"Look into the light; look close; you will see it," Michael added gently.

Sarah peered into the glowing brilliance. It was dazzling, but not too much. She squinted, and then, suddenly, she saw.

"Oh, I see it!" she giggled, captivated by the soft blue light surrounding her father.

My duck!" she breathed, then cried out, "Oh, my **wings**!"

And there they were, not a memory, but a vibrant, undeniable reality. The beloved wings of her duck, shimmering as if woven from the very fabric of starlight, more vivid, more real than anything she'd ever seen.

"What is it that you see?" Michael's voice was a gentle current in the rushing wonder, almost swallowed by the sheer spectacle. Behind him, Sarah's uncle quietly receded, his form fading into the ambient glow, leaving her utterly safe, utterly mesmerized, utterly lost in the miraculous vision unfolding before her.

"Quacker! Oh, Quacker... Oh, how I missed you," she whispered, her heart fluttering with joy.

She laughed softly as her father stepped closer, his expression warm and loving.

"Do you know how much I love you?" he asked tenderly, handing her the little duck.

Sarah held him close.

"Oh, no! I can't ever forget... I will never forget," she replied.

"Would you like to go upstairs? I will show you each step, one at a time," her dad said as they began to ascend the glowing staircase.

Then suddenly, the moment changed. Sarah was elsewhere, transported to another memory.

She moved slowly, almost floating, her body gliding like a dream. She saw herself in motion, effortless, weightless, soaring through the air that glistened like time suspended.

A horse trotted nearby, its golden mane shining under the sun.

"He's incredibly gentle," her friend said admiringly. "See? He is so gentle. Get on him."

Sarah hesitated.

"I've never ridden a horse before. Are you sure he'll like me? What if he throws me over the fence?"

"He won't throw you. Just touch him. Put your foot here, throw your leg over the top. Hold on tight and you won't fall. When you want to slow down, pull slightly on the reins. To stop, pull harder and say, 'Whoa whoa.' Got it? Are you ready?"

"Wait! I don't know if I'm ready. What if…?"

"Giddy-up!"

"Look! I'm riding him! I'm riding! Do you see me?! Are you watching me? I'm riding him!" Sarah shouted, laughter bubbling from her as she glided forward, her feet never touching the ground. But the joy was short-lived.

The world around her accelerated. The horse under her began to run faster and faster.

She searched for her friend.

Where are you? Sarah thought, scanning the endless field. No one was in sight.

Panic rose.

The horse galloped wildly. She tugged at the reins gently, then with all her strength. It wouldn't stop.

"Oh no!" she cried inwardly. "Jesus, help me! Please help me! I'm going to crash!"

The fence was close now, too close. The ground raced below her.

"Open the gate!" she screamed. "Mary! Open the gate!"

Then—impact.

Sarah fell hard, tumbling in a blur of motion. She hit the ground, dizzy and breathless. Around her, radiant droplets of color shimmered like fragments of a broken dream. A loud buzz filled her ears, and disembodied voices echoed in the distance.

"God, can you hear me?" she cried. "Where am I? These voices... where are they coming from?"

She lifted her head and saw a glowing figure of brilliant whiteness.

"Are you my angel?" she whispered, barely audible.

Her body felt heavy and numb. Her limbs wouldn't move. She lay still.

Then they were beside her.

"Hurry! Please hurry!" her friend's voice rang out. "He threw her off! He ran up to the gate and threw her off! The gate wasn't even closed! She thinks I'm an angel. Do you think she'll be okay?"

Sarah wept. Her shoulders trembled. Her tears fell freely.

Then, her father's deep voice came through, "It's alright, Sarah," he murmured, brushing her hair back. "Don't cry. Are you alright? Look at me. Are you alright?"

She tried to nod, but her body was too weak.

When his worried gaze met hers, she felt a wave of safety wrap around her like a blanket. His presence was a balm against the storm inside her.

She blinked.

And just like that, she was standing back at her father's house in heaven.

Twelve rooms stretched before her, each radiating a different, vibrant, rich, and living color.

"Each room has a door, and every door is like a gate," her father explained. "The gate can never be shut."

Angels stood guard outside every third room. Sarah listened. Weak chiming echoed softly from within each space.

"Where's the music coming from?" she wondered aloud.

Michael approached the brightly colored rooms, each one humming a unique melody.

"Each room has its own color," he explained. "Don't let them bleed together. Come on, I will show you."

Her father took her hand, leading her to one of the doors. It stood between two enormous pillars, each one carved into a towering angel.

"Look – I want you to see," her father said, reaching into his pocket. "I carved this little one in my workshop. He opened his hand, revealing a small, white angel made just for her.

Suddenly, Sarah was no longer in the hallway.

She was back at the lunch table with her fourth-grade class.

She reached toward her tray, picked up something small, and clutched it tightly. All day long, she held onto that little black olive.

When the bus dropped her off, she walked the familiar sidewalk back home. Inside, her father sat with her little brother on his lap.

Sarah clutched her treasure, waiting patiently for her turn. As soon as her brother finished sharing his schoolwork, she climbed into her father's lap.

"I have something for you," she announced proudly. "I've been holding onto it all day."

"What do you have for me?" he asked, a smile playing on his lips.

Sarah slowly opened her hand, revealing the small, dark olive. She placed it gently into his palm, and his face lit up with joy.

Just then, Sarah looked toward the door. Her sister stood there, ready to take her turn, a secret gift clutched in her own hands. Together, they both stared at the growing collection of olives in their father's open palm.

The scene by the door seemed to melt away, and in its place, a profound sense of peace washed over her as she was back in the hallway of rooms, hand-in-hand with her father. They continued walking. Music poured from every door they passed. The melodies wove together, forming a brilliant harmony that whirled around her, lifting her heart.

They entered one of the rooms, bathed in a soft, welcoming glow. When her father said, "This is your room, Sarah," she gasped.

The walls pulsed gently, alive with shades of amethyst, coral, and sky blue. But they weren't just colors. They whispered secrets, carrying stories and inviting dreams. They held her past, present, and future.

Then, just beyond the stillness, Sarah heard an angelic voice singing softly, guiding her. A butterfly appeared, its wings a tapestry of shifting patterns, alive with meaning. It floated silently in the air, its movements did were not random, but intentional. Each flutter and gentle arc was like a sentence, like a story told in the language of motion and grace. Sarah felt drawn to it. She sensed it was trying to speak to her, not with words, but through its presence.

Her gaze lifted.

The ceiling above her was a billowing canvas of cloth, forming a dreamlike glow throughout the room. Wonder bloomed in her chest. The polished cherrywood floor sparkled below her and glinted like water touched by light. In one corner stood a canopy bed, its chiffon curtains cascading down like mist, glowing softly from within, beckoning her, promising warmth, dreams, and secret comfort.

Her fingertips itched to brush the delicate fabric, to listen to whatever the soft threads were whispering.

Near the bed stood a beautiful dresser, its surface smooth and elegant, and a plush armchair nestled beside it. Every piece in the room felt like a quiet promise of rest, peace, and beauty.

Sarah looked around slowly with a swelling heart.

Her world until now had been one of faded wallpaper and shared bedrooms. Now, she stood in a space that glinted like starlight spilled across midnight velvet. The air itself felt like magic. *Home* had always meant tight spaces, hushed voices, and worn furniture for her.

But this room... this room sang a different story.

The colors weren't just hues; they were symbols—a secret language. Sarah couldn't wait to sink into that canopy bed and decode the enchantments woven into its threads.

She could only stare, completely entranced and overwhelmed,

Then, the scene transitioned.

Sarah continued onward, stepping into a space forgotten by time. A place where memories floated like whispers. Deep within her soul, her eyes captured a picture.

Her daddy's voice rose in song:

"Lollipop, Lollipop, Oh, Lolli-Lolli-Lolli, Lollipop, Lollipop. Where are the little lollipops?"

"I chose it just for you."

"Who picked the lollipop?" Sarah giggled. "Oh, Daddy, I hear them! I see them! What color is it for me?" she asked.

"Lollipop! It's you, Amber!" He sang, twirling joyfully. Michael appeared, reaching out his hands. "Look, do you see them?"

"Oh, my school papers!" Sarah giggles.

"Look at the eyes. Do you see it?"

"Where did you find it?" Sarah asked, her eyes shining.

"In the mirror, see em? Let me show you where I found em. EM. was lost in E.M.I.T.," Michael said. "What do your eyes see...T.I.M.E.?" He asked.

Sarah laughed, the sound light and free.

"Look at IT. Turn IT around and look at ME. What do your eyes see? What do your ears hear? You do see what I see."

"This time, you can show it to your mother. Tell her where you found them."

And Sarah saw—and she heard:

"I now give you time. All time.
Yesterday, today, forever, and always.
Time Then, and Time Again.
And I am... and in my hands, I hold something."

Her pulse quickened.

A voice called softly, echoing through her heart:

"Come to me, and I will show you!"

The voice was angelic, like a song sung by stars. Sarah followed it into a realm where a second could stretch into eternity. Here, time was a breath, a hush, a ripple in the fabric of the soul.

"Time then and time again," echoed through her being.

Her eyes captured another picture, a timeless imprint burned into her spirit.

When she returned to her room and was back in her body, the clock on the bedside table still read **1 a.m.**

No time had passed.

For you, Little Star.

***

Nine months after conception, on her birthday, a miracle unfolded. Sarah's son was born, emerging from the cosmic womb, inside a celestial bubble bathed in starlight.

And a melody returned to her, clear and soft:

"When you wish upon a dream, a hope, a wish, a golden gleam.
The heart's desire, a shining star, a wish fulfilled, not distant far.
A twinkling hope, a magic sight, a dream come true, a pure delight."

As the nurse placed the newborn on a small bed beside her, Sarah's eyes caught a glimpse of the nurse's notepad. She could see a small butterfly delicately drawn in the corner, its intricately detailed wings surrounded by soft, swirling lines.

The simple sketch seemed to glow with an inner light, capturing the essence of transformation and new beginnings. It was as if the butterfly had been drawn there just for her, a gentle reminder of the preciousness of the moment and the infinite possibilities ahead for Sarah and her newborn son.

"Do you see music? What does the music look like?"

A newborn's cry — a hopeful sound,

A family's joy, forever bound.

A tiny soul, a precious sight,

A future's promise, pure and bright.

But fate can change, a tragic turn,

A heart may break, a spirit yearns.

A silent note, a missed refrain,

A family's sorrow, endless pain.

A heavenly choir, a distant call,

Awaiting loved ones, one and all.

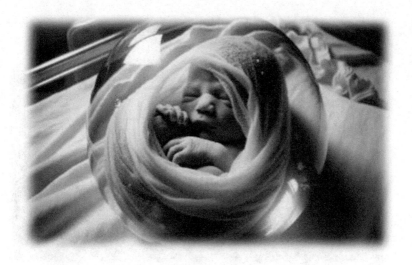

In that sacred moment, his arrival lit the delivery room.

A new soul had entered the world—a radiant being.

My son. My little star.

Epilogue

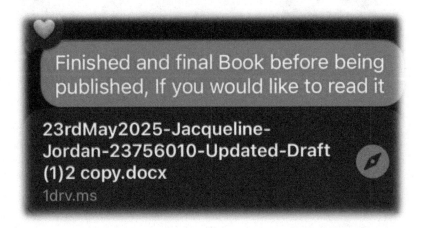

The manuscript was completed on May 23, 2025

Sarah's Birthday